May 10, 1996

Jabion and I are working our way from Camp Three up the Geneva Spur and across the yellow band of rock to Camp Four, when we are suddenly belted with an unexpected force of wind and snow. What was up to now difficult and uncomfortable now takes on a new component: danger. Every step now becomes a triumph, every minute to Camp Four increasingly painful. In the late afternoon, the wind howls through a snowstorm so intense, the snow feels like a solid wall. We manage to stumble toward the faint yellow glow of the lights coming from the tents at Camp Four. I turn away from the tents for a moment and imagine how it would feel to have only the gathering dark and snow to look at, and what courage it would take to face that empty, screeching, black night.

WITHIN REACH

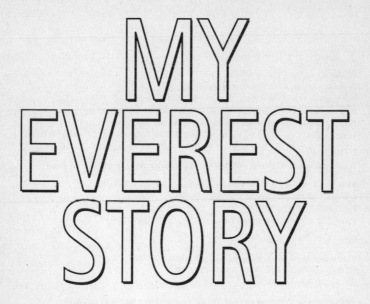

MY EVEREST STORY

MARK PFETZER & JACK GALVIN

PUFFIN BOOKS

PUFFIN BOOKS
Published by the Penguin Group
Penguin Putnam Books for Young Readers,
345 Hudson Street, New York, New York 10014, U.S.A.
Penguin Books Ltd, 27 Wrights Lane, London W8 5TZ, England
Penguin Books Australia Ltd, Ringwood, Victoria, Australia
Penguin Books Canada Ltd, 10 Alcorn Avenue, Toronto, Ontario, Canada M4V 3B2
Penguin Books (N.Z.) Ltd, 182-190 Wairau Road, Auckland 10, New Zealand

Penguin Books Ltd, Registered Offices: Harmondsworth, Middlesex, England

First published in the United States of America by Dutton Books,
a division of Penguin Books USA Inc., 1998
Published by Puffin Books,
a member of Penguin Putnam Books for Young Readers, 2000

10 9 8 7 6 5 4 3 2

THE LIBRARY OF CONGRESS HAS CATALOGED THE DUTTON EDITION AS FOLLOWS:
Pfetzer, Mark.
Within reach: my Everest story / by Mark Pfetzer and Jack Galvin.
  p. cm.
Summary: The author describes how he spent his teenage years climbing
mountains in the United States, South America, Africa, and Asia, with
an emphasis on his two expeditions up Mount Everest.
ISBN 0-525-46089-6 (hardcover)
[1. Pfetzer, Mark—Juvenile literature. 2. Mountaineers—United States—
Biography—Juvenile literature. 3. Mountaineering—Everest, Mount (China and
Nepal)—Juvenile literature. 4. Youths' writings, American. [1. Pfetzer, Mark. 2.
Mountaineers.
3. Everest, Mount (China and Nepal) 4. Youths' writings.] I. Galvin, Jack. II. Title.
GV199.92.P495A3 1998 796.52'2'092—dc21 [b] 98-29215 CIP AC

Puffin Books ISBN 0-14-130497-9

Printed in the United States of America

To Mom and Dad
—M.P.

To Maria
—J.G.

CONTENTS

MARK'S MOUNTAINS

DATE	LOCATION	HEIGHT REACHED	ACHIEVEMENT	AGE
8/94	*Mount Pisco, Peru*	19,029 ft.	Youngest to summit	14
8/94	*Huascarán, Peru*	22,205 ft.	Youngest to summit	14
12/94	*Cotopaxi, Ecuador (world's third-highest active volcano)*	19,347 ft.	Youngest to summit	14
2/95	*Aconcagua, Argentina*	22,834 ft.	Summited	15
5/95	*Mount Everest, climbed Tibet side*	25,000 ft.	Youngest on climb (titleholder—highest climb in age category)	15
8/95	*Mount Rainier, Washington*	14,410 ft.	Summited	15
10/95	*Ama Dablam, Nepal*	22,350 ft.	Youngest to summit	15

DATE	LOCATION	HEIGHT REACHED	ACHIEVEMENT	AGE
5/96	*Mount Everest, climbed Nepal side* *(surpassed previous year's record, youngest to climb 26,000 ft.)*	26,000 ft.	Youngest on climb	16
7/96	*Kilimanjaro, Africa (assistant guide)*	19,340 ft.	Summited	16
9/96	*Cho Oyu, climbed Tibet side (world's sixth-highest mountain)*	26,750 ft.	Youngest to summit	16

PREFACE

You should meet Mark Pfetzer. He's a regular kid. He answers the phone like any other kid, complains about his senior year of high school, wants a new truck, and announces new long-range plans for his life at least once a month. He's unaffected, tall, with the good looks we call clean-cut—dark trimmed hair, white teeth, clear eyes, angular nose, and a ready smile. A regular kid.

The difference is in his dreams, or should I say his dreams-to-reality ratio. Many ordinary kids have dreams. Some have big dreams. Mark seems to dream reality—regularly, as you will see in this book.

Teachers learn from students—a truism I found repeated often in my thirty years in the classroom. I learned from Mark that we can all have a healthy dreams-to-reality ratio, whether we're a thirteen-year-old junior high student, as he was, or a man in his late fifties, as I am. After working with Mark almost daily on this book for over a year, I realized the simple secret to his success. It's all in the decision. Once he decides to take on a skill or an activity, he becomes committed. Then he learns, prepares, and immerses himself so intensely that success is not only predictable but inevitable. Becoming fly-fishing champion at age nine, karate black belt at age eleven—it was all in the decision. Once made, he allows nothing to stand in his way. How else can you account for a thirteen-year-old, living in a small seaside town, with limited funds, who decides he wants to climb mountains and then finds his way to the upper reaches of Everest two years later?

I called Mark one day after he returned from Everest '96. Although we live only a mile apart, I had known about him only from newspaper accounts. He told me about breaking through an ice bridge on Mount Rainier, leaving him with nothing to stand on but a sliver of ice and 1,800 feet of air; about coughing up his soul on Everest; about dead bodies of climbers. He described standing on the highest mountains in South America, Tibet, and Nepal; the freezing landscapes of the Himalayas; the beauty of every mountain; and always the fun of putting one foot in front of the other. While his peers were hoping to make the ninth-grade basketball team or get a break from their history teacher, Mark was living a life that few could even imagine.

Aside from telling Mark's story, I knew I wanted to write this book after reading a letter he had written in the local paper following his Everest '95 trip. In the letter, he thanked all those who supported him in so many ways. He particularly thanked his father for being his best friend. He ended the letter by saying how much he loved his father—that from a fifteen-year-old, for all his friends to see!

Most of us will never climb Mount Everest, but Mark has shown us that we can all live our own adventures if we have the strength of will.

Mark, thanks for sitting still long enough for me to hear your story and for teaching me about seeking new goals, such as writing this book.

Thanks also to:

Esmond Harmsworth of Zachary Shuster Agency. Esmond was always available, attentive, and patient. His confidence in our manuscript and his tenacious energy made the publishing process satisfying and seamless.

Karen Lotz, president and publisher of Dutton Children's Books. Karen's clear editorial direction and positive affirmation of this book brought it clearly into focus.

Amy Wick, assistant editor, Dutton Children's Books. Amy's knowledge of the manuscript, her advice, suggestions, and generous good cheer during many phone calls helped bring the book to publication.

I am very grateful to the following writers for their suggestions and their expertise: Bill Goetzinger, Jim Huston, Clint Hull, Carmel McGill, Arliss Ryan, Jan Shapin, David Stone, David Tournquist, and Ron Potvin.

JACK GALVIN

ACKNOWLEDGMENTS

I wish to thank my family, friends, sponsors, fellow climbers, and all those people who have supported me over the last four years. The views I express in this account are the observations of a young climber experiencing the world's highest mountains. If I have offended anyone in the course of this narrative, I apologize.

MARK PFETZER
April 1998

NOTE: *A glossary of mountaineering terms can be found on page 223.*

within reach

MAY 9, 1996

We're on a steep section of the Lhotse Face when a group coming down from Camp Three shouts for us to get off the rope. I dig my ice ax into the 45-degree slope and watch as a climber and five Sherpas carefully lower a sled-stretcher. The bundled sleeping bag and the bit of twisted face with a froth of icy blood on its beard slide by me. "Fell at Camp Three," the climber explains. "Being unroped up there can get you killed."

"Will he be OK?" I ask.

The climber shakes his head. "Not with his internal injuries. But we gotta try."

The wind starts to pick up as we watch the stretcher's descent. At least he has a shot, I think. Lots of guys die up here, and no one even finds their bodies. Then a season or two later, a body will emerge from the snow as if it swam to the surface, still intact if its flesh hasn't been eaten by birds. There are at least four or five corpses near enough to the routes that you can see them. Maybe someone should bring them down for proper burial. But it's dangerous even to get to them. Like the rescuers who just passed us, I'd help any live climber I could. I'm not going after dead ones. Besides, climbers are left up here out of respect for their love of the mountains.

MAY 10, 1996

I always thought the tough part about climbing was, well, the climbing itself. Now, as we get into higher altitude, I'm beginning to realize that what we have to wear just makes everything so much harder. Over my down pants, jacket, and hood, I put on an oxygen mask, tank, heavy backpack, and goggles. The trouble is the mask. It has an extra-long tube to the tank, under my arms and around my back, which I keep getting twisted. I feel all tied up. Then the oxygen mask hits me just below the eyes, and the overlapping goggles stick out so far I have to bend way over just to see my feet. But if I bend over to see where I'm walking, I pinch the tube and cut off my oxygen supply. If I take the mask off, to get a breath or to spit because my cold's much worse, the rubber gets wet, and pretty soon I have inch-long icicles hanging off my chin.

Put all that into the environment of the Geneva Spur and a steep, yellow band of rock we have to traverse on the way to Camp Four, and you have high-altitude adventure. Not only do I have trouble breathing, coughing, and seeing, but now we have to angle across bald, slippery rock with crampons. Like trying to cross a steep concrete ramp on ice skates. Only it's covered with shalelike, loose rock, and when you look down, you know that if you fall, you have an express trip 5,000 feet right down the Lhotse Face. What we should be wearing are regular hiking boots with good-gripping rubber soles. But even if we had them, we couldn't risk frostbite to change. Or even take off the crampons.

Time for patience. Jabion, my Sherpa friend, and I slowly pick our way across, finding footholds for our crampons. We can hear the wind coming from above as if someone is slowly turning up the volume, and we know we'll soon be out of the protection of the Geneva Spur, and the already-swirling snow will be like needles.

Jabion and I finally get free of the Geneva Spur. We're on the long steep section, very tired, when the weather hits like a hurricane in a fog of snow. We still have one more short steep section before Camp Four, which we struggle through OK. I notice that Jabion does not have on his heavy mittens, probably thinking he wouldn't need them because he'd be in camp soon. The wind is blasting too loud for me to ask him; he must be all right.

At Camp Four, tents, maybe twenty of them erected by Sherpas and climbers already up here, are concentrated in one flat, rocky area. All the teams need and have tents up here, the final refuge before the summit, 3,000 feet away.

Camp Four is at 26,000 feet. Above 25,000 feet—known as the "Death Zone"—the temperatures and winds can be so severe, the air so thin, that climbers are in constant danger. Thinking and movement slow down; even a small error like dropping a glove can mean death, because a hand can freeze, become useless. So these tents are vital to survival. Fortunately for Jabion and me, ours are the first tents we come to. I stumble inside, get the mask off, wipe the icicles and slime off my face, and Jabion mumbles something about his hands. They are extremely white. I start yelling at him as if I'm the father and he's the little kid. "Ya shoulda said something back there!"

"Aw," he mumbles. That's all he can think of to say. Possible frostbite—the kind that costs fingers—and all he can say is "Aw"? I put his hands under my armpits for five minutes, give him a high dosage of oxygen, put his heavy mittens on, and Jabion lucks out. A half hour later he's fine. Lost in the moment is my personal altitude record: 26,000 feet. Soon we all crowd into two tents: Neil, Brigeete, Michael, and Graham in one tent. Pemba, Pasang, Jabion, Lhakpa, Ang Tshering, and me in the other. Thirty oxygen bottles, a small stove, and six guys in sleeping bags have us all jammed in. Jabion's arm sticks into my shoulder; I'm next to Pasang, who smells; and, as close as we are, the wind—the train roaring next to your ear now—drowns out the loudest shout. As strange as it may seem, I love it here in this tent. I'm relatively warm, have no headache, am breathing fairly easily, and will summit Everest tomorrow. I am ready. I have worked toward this moment since I was thirteen, climbed the highest mountains in South America, reached 25,000 feet on Everest last year, and trained very hard to be here at Camp Four. In spite of all the critics who say a sixteen-year-old has no business on Everest, I am within reach of the summit.

Funny that I should choose to be with the Sherpas, the people who live in the mountains and work as our guides, porters, and cooks. Most climbers keep their distance and have only a work relationship with them. Al Burgess introduced me to the Sherpas when I first came to Nepal three years ago, and so I learned to visit their homes, drink tea with them, help them carry equipment. They, in turn, have taught me that time means so little, that you focus on each day, get up with the sun, eat, work all day, eat, and go to bed when it gets dark.

Over the last three years, I learned what great people the Sherpas are. In fact, Jabion and I became very good friends, so much so that I promised I'd take him to America for the summer after this trip. I already have his visa arranged. The other Sherpas have their orders in for hats and T-shirts. About five o'clock, Neil comes in from the other tent and shouts above the wind, "Henry radioed. Says some of Scott Fischer's climbers might be missing." While we are having difficulty being heard, keeping warm, and eating limp noodles, there are climbers outside in this wind!

Neil's back soon. "Now Henry says Ray's missing!" A veteran climber once told me that one of the most important pieces of equipment a climber uses on Everest is the two-way radio. By calling back and forth, Base Camp people and their climbers, who are spread all over the mountain, can exchange important information about conditions and positions. Our two-way radio has become a lifeline.

Jabion and Pemba bundle up, put on headlamps, and head out into the dark to look for Ray. They will follow the trail down toward Camp Three and hope to find him safely tucked behind a rock. They are soon back. "Can't see." Jabion points to his lamp. We all know what he means: the snow is coming horizontally, so hard that a headlamp is useless, as are the dark lenses of the goggles at night. Without goggles they risk taking the needlelike snow directly at the eyes.

The night goes on, and we have no idea what may be happening outside. As time goes along, we do know that anyone stuck out there will have at least nine more hours of pitch dark, snow driven by winds over a hundred miles an hour, and windchill near a hundred below. We doze, we eat, we drink, and slowly all the inevitable questions seep in. Is this just one storm? Has the window of opportunity closed? Are there people hurt? Dead? None of us huddled in our tent know the answers. I begin to feel my cough steal away more and more of my strength. I have to summit soon, before I lose my strength. We're so close—within reach—and all we can do is hang on to this scab of rocks, 26,000 feet up, and hope that daylight will give us new hope to reach our goal.

CHAPTER ONE getting started

What's a carabiner? Dynamic rope? Static rope? How do you put on a harness? I'm twelve years old, waiting my turn to go up a 40-foot rock, scared to death. We're at the Alton Jones Wilderness Center at the University of Rhode Island for an advanced camping trip—hiking, camping, and this one day of rock climbing. I squint through the sunshine up the rock face. Bet I could make it easy, just run up there. But all those ropes. Must be more dangerous than it looks.

It's all Christian's fault. He's the director. He said I could do the advanced course, even though I'm a seventh grader, three years younger than the others. Not smaller, just younger. He also said I did well in basic camping week, that I was mature, took on extra duties, tried hard, helped out, was ready for advanced. So now I'm facing this wall and don't feel at all advanced. The other guys don't know I'm twelve, but it's going to show now!

"You have to lean back in the rope," Alex yells up to me. Easy for him to say. He's so wiry he floats up the rock face as if he's walking on a beach. I lean back and try to smile. This is a stupid way to get hurt! I can't believe my parents let me do this. I know the harness is going to break. It can't be right, to lean back, to trust a rope.

But I do. And find places to put my feet. And pull my weight up. Before I know it, I'm on top! I'm up! Try to be cool, Mark. Stop laughing like a little kid. What a feeling! There's this rock. I want to go up this rock. And I do! Simple. God, this is fun. I'm still shaking inside, but it is fun. Until the rappel. We move to another side to get back down. Going down has to be easier, right? Wrong. You have to face the rock and lean out backward, step back, lower your butt, and let your center of gravity go, like doing a back dive from 40 feet with no water below. You have to just let it go, a weird feeling of losing control. So I let go.

Come on, legs, quit shaking. Just lower your butt and just walk down. Nothing to it. All I need is a few more steps and I'm down. I go from scared to happy, from death to life. I make it. All I have to do is step backward into air, lean into the unknown, then feel the harness. Legs still shake; I'm gulping for air, but so what? I make it.

And I love it. Something about it won't let me go. Maybe it's because my own arms and legs and mind are doing something hard to do. Maybe that's it. Going up and down because I can.

So different from ball sports. I found out I never liked them at all. Football, basketball, even baseball. I'm big enough. But I like endurance sports. Hiking, running, lifting weights. And fly-fishing, bluefishing tournaments, casting tournaments, making flies for people and selling them to bait shops. Hunting.

I like working on a goal, making it happen. Karate, for instance. I got my black belt last year—a lot of work, but fun perfecting the moves, learning discipline and patience. Making fishing flies, same thing. Discipline and patience. When I was nine, I loved to sit for hours working with bits of animal fur and plastic to make them look real.

Trouble is, not many kids my age like hunting and fishing, so most of my friends are older. Chuck, for instance, my best hunting and fishing buddy, is fifty-three. Seems funny, doesn't it? A twelve-year-old kid hanging out with an old guy? I even spent a lot of time with my grandfather and his friends, fishing. I could sit for hours and talk with them. Sometimes kids my age like to fool around a lot, but I never liked that. So I hung out with older people—from their thirties to seventies.

OCTOBER 1993

I'm too young for the RI Rock Gym. You're supposed to be at least fifteen. But I can't wait two years. Ever since this past summer, when I climbed again at Alton Jones, I've been reading about climbing and trying to figure out how to learn more. I saw an ad about an indoor climbing place in Pawtucket. When I called, I was told I had to be fifteen. I end up in a rock gym in Waterbury, Connecticut, instead. My parents are willing to drive me once or twice a week, but it is very far away, almost two hours each way, so we also show up one day at the RI Rock Gym, which is only forty-five minutes away. By now I have my harness and climbing shoes, know the knots and belaying techniques, and because I look fifteen, they don't ask and I don't tell.

The inside of a rock gym is weird. Outside it looks like an ordinary building, which it is. Not even that high. Inside, it's floor-to-ceiling bumpy walls, with overhangs and ropes hanging down, gravel for a floor, and people trying to go up these walls, only 30, maybe 40 feet high at most, hanging on to little handholds sticking out a bit from the bumps so you can almost get a grip. Rock gyms are not very high. Not even dangerous. Because you are roped in, you can always be safely lowered, if and when you let go.

Trying to get up a rock-gym wall can drive you crazy, though. Those little bumps and angles stretch your arms, and particularly your legs, into funny positions, and the little handholds can be torture on the routes those guys devise. So you can pretend you're 3,000 feet up some vertical cliff, with the wind howling in your ears, and you have only this tiny crack of a handhold and you have to put your weight onto it so you can shift your weight from leg to leg. So you pull yourself up to an overhang, and you go out a bit farther. The wind is worse, and a bird flies by—your hands are really numb now, and your nose suddenly gets itchy, and you don't dare scratch it (being 3,000 feet up in the wind), but it's driving you crazy. You try to wiggle your face around, even scratch against the wall, but it gets worse. You have no choice but to let go and scratch it. And so you do. You let go. But it's OK; it's only pretend. You're on belay, inside a rock gym. With a vivid imagination.

NOVEMBER 8, 1993

I go more and more to the rock gym, feel my arms and legs get stronger, feel my fingers get tough, able to hold my weight more and more. The routes up the wall start to look like ladders to me—ladders with all kinds of crazy steps, but ladders. If you are patient enough to figure them out, that'll get you to the top.

I'm watching this tall skinny guy who goes up the wall as if he's glued to it, as if his route's a real ladder with easy steps. All his moves are silky, easy, without any waste. I can't help but watch him. Someone tells me his name: Geoff Tabin, a doctor who's climbed all over the world, a guy who's already climbed to the top of Mount Everest, a guy with a million stories to tell about mountain climbing. I go up on the wall near him; we start to talk. I tell him I'm very interested in climbing. He's working around a very long stretch between handholds. He asks me how old I am. I'm trying to get over a small bump, trying to find a handhold. I whisper that I'm thirteen. "Thirteen!" He yells out so loud, Jimmy, the guy in charge of the gym, looks up suspiciously. "Big for thirteen." He laughs, pulls himself up, looks down at Jimmy. "Got by him? Guess you do want to climb."

We become good friends after that, the doctor who climbs walls and the thirteen-year-old kid. Geoff never stops talking. Every time we meet to climb at the rock gym, I learn something new about climbing the big mountains, about Nepal, Tibet, the Himalayas, the deep valleys, the mountainside Buddhist monasteries, the dirt-poor Nepali people, who smile all day with so little to smile about. All this while I'm struggling to go up a route next to Geoff, who's talking away as if we're sitting at the kitchen table.

Soon we *are* sitting at a kitchen table. My parents invite Geoff and his girlfriend to dinner one night. He doesn't bring slides or videotapes, but he might as well have, because his words fill my mind with all kinds of pictures of climbing the highest mountains in the world, of going to far-off places, of standing on the summit of Mount Everest. Here's a guy sitting at my own kitchen table who's making his adventures sound like so much fun, and he's a doctor, too, doing important medical work. While we are having dessert (chocolate cake with white frosting, my favorite), and Geoff is laughing about his memory of riding in a truck up a muddy mountain pass with the wheels two inches from a 2,000-foot drop, my mind is at work and it's saying to me: "You're gonna do that someday. When you're Geoff's age, you're gonna have all the same stories, only better. And be a doctor, too."

"You ought to try ice climbing. You're ready for something challenging," Geoff says to me one night as we coil rope in the rock gym. "Get some instruction in ice climbing if you really want to climb."

"Yeah? How do I pay?"

"Get a sponsor. A lot of climbing people do. Someone willing to help you pay for it."

"Who'd want to, I mean, pay for a thirteen-year-old?"

Geoff just laughs. "You want to go? You'll get there."

I learn quickly that Geoff's right—you have to work at it if you want to get there, because no one's going to hand it to you. I find out my aunt's music teacher used to climb, so I call him to find out about ice climbing. He only hikes, he says, too old for ice climbing. Three or four more calls and I'm in touch with an ice-climbing instructor who wants me to see him in December. Finally it's settled: Lake Placid in December; cost—$300. One small question bothers me: where am I going to get $300?

I write a letter to Roger Grady, the owner of the Newport Athletic Club, where I work out, and I tell him I'm a kid who wants to pursue physical fitness through climbing, and I'd like to take a course in ice climbing, and it costs $300 and could he help. Boy, does he help. All $300! With a nice note saying how glad he is to see a kid my age so interested in physical fitness. I have the money to go. Just like that!

NOVEMBER 1993

Good thing I made all those phone calls about ice climbing. My aunt's music teacher calls back and says I'd better spend some time in the mountains before I take on ice climbing. He's right; I've never even seen a mountain. Because he's such a good friend of my aunt, he's willing to take me, even willing to come down to pick me up. I find out he is a famous musical conductor, Francis Madeira, who founded the Rhode Island Philharmonic, now retired in Maine. I don't know what to expect from Mr. Madeira. I know he's promised to take me to some mountains in New Hampshire. I also know he's seventy-seven years old, so we'll probably just drive around and walk a little. At least I'll see mountains, if only from a car.

Am I wrong about Frank! (That's what he wants me to call him.) Picture a wiry, lean young man who walks so fast, you feel like a little kid trying to keep up. Now put him on a mountain hiking trail, with a backpack and a smile for every living thing he sees out there, and finally, put an old man's lined, craggy, straight-jawed face on him, and you have Frank. Seventy-seven! I thought you took it easy at seventy-seven. Not Frank. He's out on the mountains every chance he gets. Over to the Alps twice a year. Up Mount Washington. This guy doesn't have blood in his veins, he has electricity!

We hike Mount Crawford with a group of people. It's a clear, cold day, and I can see why Frank loves it so much. We stop to admire the view that goes on and on for miles. I can feel the still, cold mountain air gradually warm in the weak November sun, but a hint of winter is in the bare trees, a light snow covers the quiet hiking trail. We get to the top of Mount Crawford, and I can feel my legs get a sweet, tired feeling from the effort of getting here and feel also a sense of happiness, triumph, victory, for making it.

From where I stand, I can see peaks all around us, some close, some miles away, but all suddenly available to me. If I can climb one, I know I can climb them all. Now I know what those surfers at the beach near my house feel when they see a high surf. All those waves, just coming and coming, and they want to ride every one. That's the way my first view of the mountains hits me: all those mountains—I want to ride every one!

To celebrate our ascent, Frank offers me his thermos of hot beef bouillon. God, is it awful! It tastes disgusting, but I can't let him know that. I focus, instead, on how much I feel at home up here, as much as the two hawks gliding on the thermals above us seem to be.

It's hard to explain, but I know I have found a place where I'm going to want to spend a lot of time.

Later at dinner in his condo, Frank tells me about classical music; about his wife, Jean, who was a soprano with the Metropolitan Opera in New York, who died so young; about piano; and about his hearing problem. A whole life devoted to music, and he can hardly hear it anymore. But he isn't whining. Just telling me. I can hear the passion in his voice when he talks about music, and I picture him in a tuxedo, in front of the RI Philharmonic, making a deep bow after a great performance. Dinner, by the way, seems pretty formal, considering we're just two guys back from hiking. I have to make sure to use the right fork and sit up straight and use proper manners, otherwise I hear about it from Frank. He's not grumpy exactly, just wants things done the right way.

Old guys are like that sometimes, but if you are willing to listen to them you can learn a lot. In one weekend I learn about classical music, the Alps, good table manners, and, most important, about hiking with a backpack in the mountains. All from a man whom most kids my age would blow off because he's too old.

finding a way

CHAPTER TWO

DECEMBER 2, 1993

My father bought me *Second Ascent*, a book about a climber who lost his legs and still climbed. Read it in two days. Mountains and climbing are starting to creep into my mind all the time. I wonder what it must be like in those huge mountains I've seen in *National Geographic*. What do you do on a trek? How do you get there? Farthest I've ever been is Kentucky.

Right now it's ten-thirty, and I can't sleep. An ad in *Outside* magazine won't let me go. Nepal trek—three weeks—March— $5,000. Would they let a thirteen-year-old kid go? I remember Geoff talking so much about the Himalayas, how I promised myself I'd go when I was his age. Now I know there's just no way I can wait till I'm Geoff's age to go to Nepal. I have to do it now. But how can I get out of school in March? For three weeks? Where would I get $5,000, anyway? Three hundred dollars is one thing, but $5,000? My parents would probably never let me go. I try to sleep, but the ad keeps me awake, like a fly buzzing around my head.

I go into my parents' room. They're already asleep.

"Mom?"

"What, Mark?"

"Can I ask you a question?"

"Tomorrow, Mark. Go back to bed."

"One quick question. Can I go to Nepal?"

A pause. "Where? Nepal? Only Nepal?"

"Those mountains. I gotta see those mountains. There's this trek." Then I tell her how much it costs.

Another pause. A yawn or a sigh. "Go back to bed."

"I can't sleep. I keep thinking about Nepal."

"OK. If you come up with the money, you can go to Nepal. Now go back to bed."

Five thousand dollars, myself? How's a thirteen-year-old kid going to do that? Walking to Nepal sounds easier. Climbing Mount Everest sounds easier. She's not saying no, but she might as well say no. I'll probably forget the whole thing—that's what she thinks, anyway.

But I have a plan. Geoff said if you want to go badly enough, you can get sponsors somehow. Here's what I do: I look through the Yellow Pages and pick out one hundred names of businesses in the Newport area. Then I write each of them the same letter. Here's part of it:

The principal of my school feels that the trip will be far more educational than three weeks in school. . . . I will learn Eastern culture firsthand, trek through valleys, see plants and animals most people only read about. . . . I will learn responsibility and teamwork. Although I have the full support of my family, the total cost is too much for my parents. . . . I'm seeking any type of financial help, no matter how small.

I make a bunch of copies, put them all in envelopes, address the envelopes, and mail them out. One hundred letters! Even one to Arnold Schwarzenegger, who's in Newport shooting scenes for *True Lies*. I'm so sure I'll get enough sponsors, I call Alan Burgess, the man leading the trek, to find out more about it. A trek is hiking and some climbing, and it takes over twenty-four hours to fly to Nepal, and, yes, he'd take a thirteen-year-old kid, if I want to go. Do I ever want to go, I tell him. Sign me up! (Without so much as a dollar to my name.)

DECEMBER 15, 1993

It works! The letter works! Almost every day the mailman is kind enough to bring me three or four letters with checks in them. "Good luck, Mark," the letters all say, glad that it seems I'm going, happy someone can do the things they always wanted to do! I can't believe that so many businesses are willing to sponsor a kid they don't know on a trip to Nepal. Almost every day for two weeks straight, I get one or two checks, sometimes more, which I wave in front of my mother's wide eyes. Before I know it I have over $4,000 in my account, like an early Christmas present, and my parents' growing confidence in a trip they never thought was possible. I just hope I can thank them all well enough. I call Al Burgess to make specific arrangements, to tell him I'm going to Nepal!

JANUARY 24, 1994

Imagine walking on an icy sidewalk, the kind that is covered with snow that has melted and then frozen again, so it's all bumpy and rough. Now turn that sidewalk so that it's going almost straight up to the sky, and you have some idea of ice climbing. My instructor has me halfway up a 200-foot frozen waterfall, on belay, and its 20 degrees and windy at Lake Placid, New York, where I am on my first outdoor climb. I kick my crampon into the ice three, four times before it holds.

"Lean into the ice! Get those heels down!"

Just the opposite of what my instincts tell me to do. But if I go on my toes, my calves start to cramp. If I lean back, all my weight goes back to my calves, making it worse. The instructor's right. Your points stay in better, your center of gravity is better, even if you feel that you're going to fall backward.

Ice climbing is slow, patient going. Two hundred feet can take you three, four hours, because you have to set anchors with ice screws, then belay stations, then clip onto an anchored rope, then climb up by using your ice ax and crampons, then come off belay, get the ice screws, rerack your rope, and start all over again. With the wind tearing at your face.

Weird things can happen ice climbing. You can break through the wet ice of a waterfall and fall into the water and drown. Or, more common, you can "dinnerplate" your way into real trouble. Dinnerplating is when you pound your ax in very hard and all the brittle ice around the blade just fractures, as if you were to pound a nail into a dinner plate. Dinnerplating leaves you without any grip at all. One veteran ice climber, going up Mount Washington one winter, put an ice screw in, and all the ice around him was so hard and brittle the whole wall dinnerplated. He fell 600 feet into powder, then tumbled 1,400 feet more. He was in a coma for three months, came out speaking in math language, because he's an engineer.

I'm very careful about dinnerplating.

As we re-rack—exchange our safety equipment—I'm surprised how warm I feel. Well, I should, with all the polypropylene stuff I have on the outside, and the adrenaline on the inside. I look down at my mother and aunt in the parking lot below, wrapped in blankets, trying to take pictures of my first climb. They can't be warm at all. I have to admit, I'm glad she's there, that she was willing to take me here. Most parents probably wouldn't let their kids get into climbing, particularly ice climbing. But my parents say as long as I get professional teachers, good equipment, train hard, and don't take unnecessary risks, they'll let me climb. There really are few risks if you are well prepared and learn patience. I also think my father likes me to have the opportunities he never had.

Dad was the second oldest of seven kids; his father died from a Christmas-night fall when Dad was eight. Grandma was left with seven kids under ten and a developing, severe rheumatoid-arthritis condition. Dad left home to join the navy at seventeen and worked hard ever since. He wanted my sister, Amy, and me to experience all the things he could never do, to be the father he never had. So I'm very lucky: I have a father who always cares about everything I do, who wants me to experience all the things he could not, who loves me just because I'm his son.

I wave down to my mother, but she and my aunt are walking back to the car to get warm. I have to admit I really like ice climbing. I love the feeling of burying my ice ax, that solid chunk sound, kicking into the smooth ice, the challenge of finding a route, a natural edge, a way up the sheer glassy ice, the cold, the wind. I love it all.

My instructor has lots of practical advice, teaches me everything from monkey hangs (so I can rest against my ice ax) to an efficient kicking technique so I get my crampon tips into the ice on the first kick rather than the fourth. After three days of work with him, I feel confident, even enjoy rappelling, because you can practically dance down the ice, sticking in your toes like some kind of ballet dancer. One thing for sure. I have a lot more confidence about Nepal than I did before I met the ice floes of Lake Placid.

CHAPTER THREE to nepal

If you ever want to get your teachers to let you out of school for three weeks to go to Nepal, have your mother do all the talking. Mine talked to the guidance counselor, who discussed it with the teachers, who thought I'd learn more in three weeks in Nepal than I would at home, gave me assignments, and wished me luck. Easy. Nothing to it. As long as your mother is a good talker. As long as you promise to keep up with your work.

I don't tell many people at school I'm even going to Nepal. My older fishing buddies, I tell them everything about the trip, but kids my age, I just tell them I'm going away. They don't ask; I don't tell. Don't want to look as if I'm showing off, so I just keep my mouth shut.

When I finally leave, actually get on the plane in Boston, I don't even wave back to my parents. They're yelling at me to be careful and waving like crazy, and I act as if I don't even know them. They spend weeks getting me ready, helping me in every way, drive me everywhere I have to go, including the airport, and I don't even wave. The trouble is, I'm so focused on where I'm going, I block everything else out. I am focused on getting to Salt Lake City, then Los Angeles, then Korea, then Thailand, then Kathmandu, then hiking and climbing the mountains of the Langtang region of Nepal. And I've never even been on a plane before!

MARCH 3, 1994

"What kind of crampons do you use?" I ask Alan Burgess, the leader of the trek, sitting next to me on our thirteen-hour flight from Los Angeles to Seoul, Korea. He doesn't answer because he seems to be asleep. My RI Rock Gym friend, Geoff Tabin, in his book, *Blind Corners*, makes Al and his twin brother, Adrian, seem like big, wild, adventurous English guys who've been traveling and climbing full-time all over the world for over twenty years, staying alive by their quick thinking on and off the mountains. Geoff writes about them escaping from robbers and making deals to stay alive as much as he writes about their climbing. What I see is a thin man (stays in shape by cross-country skiing *up* mountains), about forty-five, with a long blond ponytail, tons of wrinkles from being on the mountains so long, and a complete inability to sit still—except on planes. Get him in a plane seat, and he can't keep awake.

"How come those titanium ice screws cost so much?" I can't help myself. The questions just fall out of my mouth. There's so much I want to ask him.

He opens one eye. "Get some Russian ones in Kathmandu. Only six bucks. Almost as good."

We're in the last row. We're watching movies, eating, sleeping, eating again, things we do every day, only the whole time we're about 30,000 feet over the Pacific. I'm finally starting to relax. Boston to Salt Lake City, then next day to L.A. International Airport, where they speak about thirty languages over the PA system, and people run in every direction, and you think you're in some foreign place. Scared me, I have to admit. I have to come back this way by myself. No Al to drag me like a little kid to the right place. I know what's going to happen. I'm going to make it halfway around the world and back, and then get lost in L.A. Airport. They'll find my body three months later, after I've starved to death looking for my plane to Boston.

"What's better, single or double ropes?"

Al opens the other eye. "Double." Al and Adrian learned to climb on the limestone cliffs in Yorkshire, England, and both have traveled the world ever since. Al guides treks to Nepal ten months a year. Doesn't make much money, but he loves the mountains, knows the Nepali people, their religions, their culture, and seems a bit crazy.

"Any ice climbing in Kathmandu?"

Both eyes are closed. "Nope."

MARCH 4, 1994

We're running into the terminal in Bangkok, Thailand, Al telling me to hurry. He's been here many times, knows what to do. What we're running for is to beat everyone else off the plane to get to the day rooms. We have twelve hours here. If we can get a day room with beds and shower and private bath, we can get some normal sleep; otherwise we sit on hard seats in the waiting area. Or take a cab into Bangkok and take a chance on missing the plane.

MARCH 4 or 5, 1994

I have no idea what day it is, or even what time it is. I've been in the air so long everything seems out of focus, fuzzy. We spent twelve hours in Bangkok, trying to sleep, walking around the airport, then back on the plane for our last leg, another five hours. The whole time Al told me stories of stealing back his own money from black-market thieves in Peru, and giving an obnoxious Pakistani government "official" antidiarrhea medication in his food for two weeks. The guy never knew what his problem was, finally slunk off before he took his "cut" of money. By now I have no more questions for Al; I wish I had waved good-bye to my parents; I'd love to be in my own bed. Now!

Al nudges me, as the plane seems to be turning. "Look. There's Everest." As the plane banks, I can see a white hump off in the distance rising out of a nest of other humps. The Himalayas. They seem small, manageable from this height and distance. I watch them slide by the window as the plane banks toward Kathmandu, and I realize that I will soon be in those mountains, the highest in the world! Then, it seems, in minutes we're on the ground, running again, Al dancing his way through the visa line, then customs. The languages and chaos of people same as L.A. Airport, only louder, faster. "Make sure you tell them your equipment's only for trekking—not for climbing." Al sweats it out as they start to look at my duffel—half full of my stuff, half full of Al's food supplies for his K2 climb later in the spring. If he's caught, it's all confiscated. Al will have to buy all new food, at very high prices. And if they think we're climbing the high mountains instead of hiking around, they'd get us for a very expensive license. The customs man looks me over, waves me through, Al behind, trying not to smile.

Then out on the street, where kids my age try to grab our stuff, supposedly to bring it to our hotel, but it seems like they're all stealing it, running in opposite directions, screaming. I want to chase after my duffel, but Al throws me into a cab, which seems to be going the wrong way on a one-way street—people honking and screaming at the driver, who's honking back and screaming, winding his way through oncoming traffic. I see other cars and cabs doing the same thing. This isn't one-way. It isn't any way. People just drive, make up their own lanes, and blow their horns. A cow sits right in front of us. Dogs swirl around, barking, snarling. A water buffalo strolls slowly across our path. We pass men who look like Native Americans only much smaller, struggling with loads like file cabinets, or huge boxes, or pieces of furniture on their backs, supported only by a head strap. Darker men, maybe from India, ride bicycles, selling bananas and limes and pineapples. Or Tiger Balm and imitation Swiss Army knives. Other riders, little guys, pull rickshas carrying big Americans. Every horn on every car and bike is blaring New Year's Eve–style all the time, even if no one's in the way.

And the smells just about knock me over: human waste, cow dung, trash left on the side of the street to rot, cooking food, combined with a thick fog of dust, smoke, and car fumes—rolling at us in hot waves.

Could this be Kathmandu? Where are all the people who are supposed to sit around on beautiful rugs in the clear mountain air? All I see are big buildings, and traffic jams, and stink! We drive by the Royal Palace, which is more like what I thought it would be, beautiful buildings and green grass and trees. Even there, they have strange huge bats hanging upside down from the limbs of most trees.

Kathmandu plays over and over inside my eyelids when I try to sleep at our hotel. I still have no idea what time it is here, or even what day. Or when I should eat or get up. I do know I wish I'd waved good-bye to my parents, wish I could see and hear and smell the ocean a mile from my house.

The next day's better. We eat at an Indian restaurant, The Third Eye, where you sit on mats on the floor and eat delicious, unleavened nan bread. I meet Eric and Hillary, the only other two trekkers on our trip. They're from California, in their mid-twenties, and fun to wander around Kathmandu with. Most trekking groups are larger than ours, some up to fifteen. We're lucky to be this small.

Al is so busy hiring Sherpas and organizing transportation, I see him very little until he introduces me to *daal bhat takari*. Al knows a painter, Kama Lama, who does intricate, religious paintings with gold leaf and ground stone dust. We get talking, and Kama invites us to lunch at his home—a little house with dirty windows and little benches, and a mouse running around the floor. We have *daal bhat takari* (lentils, rice, and curried vegetables) for lunch. I have trouble with curry, but to be polite, I finish what's on my plate. Kama brings me another plateful, which I also eat—Frank Madeira would be proud of my good manners—and then buffalo curd, a watery yogurt with coconut in it. We talk about Kama's paintings and the mountains, and I go back to the hotel just in time to be sick for two days.

MARCH 9, 1994

Al and I are sitting in the front seat of the bus. Directly over us is the one loudspeaker, blaring out a sort of folk-rock Nepali song. The girl's voice is shrill, awful, made worse by static from the speaker. Next to us are Eric and Hillary. Behind Hillary and Eric sit our Sherpas.

Sherpa is actually the family name of the Nepali people who work most with climbers and trekkers. They live in the mountains and are a very hardworking, simple people. Jabion is our sirdar, or leader. Lhakpa is the cook, and Phurba is his kitchen helper. Pemba and Kami are porters/kitchen helpers.

It's five-thirty A.M. and everyone is quiet. The Sherpas are staring at me, checking me out, trying to figure out what a young kid's doing here. I can feel their unblinking eyes on my back. But I don't care. I no longer have diarrhea, but I can eat very little. Every move

I make is a big effort. Loading the bus this morning seemed like the most difficult thing I had ever done. Don't want to whine, though. Keep it to myself. Content just to sit here and look out at the world.

We pass dirty little towns, farther and farther from Kathmandu, into open and higher country. We see all kinds of strange things: a man with six toes, an albino girl, a fallen boulder that someone made a house around, an airstrip in the middle of nowhere, and, wherever there's a little space of dirt on the side of the mountain, terracing. The hills are so steep that the farmers dig out sections of the hills and make them flat like a terrace, so they can plant potatoes, barley, and rice. Every bit of usable land becomes important, so you can see a whole series of terraces connected by walkways. From a distance they seem like different shades of green patchwork on the sides of the mountains, as if a giant had been playing in the dirt and came up with a neat design.

The higher the bus gets, the narrower the road. I look out the window and see far down the drop-off, and look up and see nothing but rock. But I'm not nervous. Our driver is very cautious, meaning that he leans on his horn at every sharp curve. He never slows down, never hits the brake, never seems concerned about a head-on collision with a bus or truck, even though there's not enough room for two to pass without one being edged down that drop-off. We see the rusted carcasses of rolled-over buses to prove it. The driver, crazed look in his eye, just hits the horn and makes good time.

And I love it. For some reason my stomach feels better with every corner. With every new view. I wonder how the passengers on top of the bus feel, hanging on for their lives as we swerve along, up and down switchbacks and mountain passes. God, is it fun! Our driver may be crazy, but he's smart. There's no right-of-way here. He takes the inside, hugs the mountain, and if someone comes the other way, the other driver has to go to the outside, the edge. A bus comes down. Both of us lurch to a stop, then like huge elephants sniffing each other, we inch by, with little kids banging on the sides of the buses to signal directions. After all, they have no rearview mirrors.

After eight such hours, we reach the Langtang region, which is clear blue sky and a flat plateau of beautiful scenery. We set up our tents, and Al delivers a sermon on always washing our hands in *pinki pani* (pink disinfectant) before we eat. And then, because we're getting up in altitude, he gives us a pill called Diamox, which helps maintain the fluid balance in the body, helps control altitude sickness, which can be a real problem for some people. You can get headaches, nosebleeds, and, when it gets really bad, pulmonary edema, where you can actually die as your lungs fill up with fluid. I am sure to take my pill! (Pills are one precaution, shots are another. Before I could even leave for Nepal, I had to have shots right in my butt—from some needles as thick as nails—for tetanus, hepatitis B, meningococcal meningitis, and typhoid.)

MARCH 16, 1994

We hike along an old trading route, the only connection that existed among the mountain villages for hundreds of years. In the United States, most of the old stuff we see in museums, or even preserved as antiques, reminds us of what life must have been like. And we think that it's kind of neat to still have it around. But here, the five-hundred-year-old trails are not just a preserved bit of history; they're still the only way to get around.

The trail is well kept, and we are able to hike five to nine miles a day, a lot considering the altitude and the pack I carry. I'm still feeling weak, so I get behind the others. Pasang Sherpa often walks with me, and we'll quietly walk along, watching the monkeys fling themselves through the trees, or go through a bamboo forest, where it's muggy and dark and very green. Sometimes we stop in a village tearoom, later feeling the sun warm as we walk higher and higher into the mountains.

I have to admit, it is not very hard work. Especially when you start to get hungry around noontime and you walk around a corner and there it is, like a mirage in the desert—the tents set up and a good lunch served by the Sherpas. Around four or five, we stop for the day. The tents are set up again, tea and biscuits are served, and dinner is cooking. It's like having your home moving always just ahead of you, always ready when you need it. The Sherpas are always way ahead of us, smiling, as if this were the easiest thing in the world to do.

The Sherpas no longer stare at me. Now they tease me, teach me their card games, their language, and laugh when they try to offer me cigarettes. They all seem to smoke themselves and think nothing of sitting in a smoky, unventilated room. Geoff told me about one Sherpa he saw on Everest who took the world's highest cigarette break at 26,000 feet. They must be healthy, though, because they can climb with remarkable loads, have terrific teeth, and never seem to get tired. I do. Get tired. And I have problems sleeping. Anybody would, with Al in the next tent snoring so loud you think he's in your ear. And through his snores I can hear the yak bells going all night like alarm clocks. Yaks are like cows. Only hairier, uglier. Sherpas use them to carry loads in the mountains, because they survive best over 9,000 feet. We have some with us. They all have bells that are like cowbells. For some reason, a yak likes to cuddle up outside my tent at night. It's like having an alarm clock the size of a huge buffalo constantly going off next to you. No matter how calm the wind, no matter how still the yak, the bell continues to make a noise, as if it's on its own battery. Why does the yak pick my tent? I want to shoo the yak away, but it won't do any good, I can tell.

Other than that, we all seem to be acclimatized pretty well. If you want to call sticking your head in an ice-cold mountain stream to wash your hair acclimatized. Al, Hillary, and Eric do it. Not me! I'll go without a shower for twenty days if I have to.

MARCH 20, 1994

We set up camp in Kyangjin Gompa, our base for our two summit tries: Nya Kanga, a 19,000-foot peak, and Yala Peak, a little lower. I can tell we're up pretty high already. When I go into a small tea-house at Trilley Lama and order my first Coke in a long time, the carbonation goes right up my nose!

Al wants to climb Tsergo Ri first for practice at altitude. It's 16,000 feet high, and we scramble to get up to the summit, but we make it—my first ascent in the Himalayas. It's a great feeling to be standing up there in the cold sunshine, knowing that I'm so far above anything I could ever climb back in New England. After all, Mount Crawford, the only mountain I've ever really climbed, is under 4,000 feet, and Mount Washington, the highest on the East Coast, is not even 6,000. From where I'm standing, I'd be 10,000 feet above everything else at home, but here I look up to so many peaks, with Mount Everest, off in the distance, 13,000 feet higher still.

MARCH 22, 1994

Yala Base Camp is beautiful, a flat, grassy meadow with trees and a stream and warm sunshine, just like the pictures you see of the Rockies in ads for sports vans. You know, the camp all set up, the father smiling at the mother, while the two kids sit around the fire and the trusty sports-utility vehicle waits like a patient yak or something. Anyway, it is well worth the two days of hiking up from Kyangjin Gompa to get here. What a surprise to find my tent covered with snow in the morning! So much snow that we have to "post hole" our way through the thigh-deep drifts to get to the base of Yala Peak. Al, Hillary, Eric, Jabion, and I all carry heavy packs of ropes, harnesses, crampons, and supplies that, combined with the deep snow, turn Yala into a challenge I didn't expect.

MARCH 24, 1994

Hiking back, retracing our steps, I realize how sick I was on the way up. I feel much stronger now; I even race Lhakpa down a long stretch of trail. But I can't keep up with him. I don't know why. He's so much older, smokes. I should beat him. Maybe I'm laughing too much, or maybe Lhakpa has downhill momentum on his side. After all, he's carrying a full load of heavy kitchen equipment, while I have only a light pack.

We end up near Kathmandu, at a lake where the statue of the Sleeping Vishnu sits in the water. Al tells us that Vishnu is believed to be the protector of the universe, and people have been coming here for over five hundred years to pray for her protection. The statue is wooden, lapped over by the dirty water of the lake, yet somehow preserved all this time. Tradition says that huge serpents lived in the lake and would eat people during flooding monsoons. Hundreds of people still come every Saturday with flowers to pray for Vishnu's protection against the serpent. I had never seen such a ritual before, and I was lucky to witness so many people still treating an ancient tradition with the same great respect their ancestors probably had.

MARCH 27, 1994

Al and I are standing on a roaring street in Kathmandu saying good-bye. He hands me a list of airports and directions and strategies about customs: find a pretty girl to focus on, watch her go through, because if customs people see you sweating bullets, they'll search you every time. I interrupt him and start asking him about Everest, about his trips there, about what it's like. "Why?" Al wants to know.

"Just curious." He'd almost summited Everest without supplemental oxygen, experienced it all. I don't know why I pick now to ask him; all that time on the trek and I have to start right now, as a van's waiting to take me to the airport.

Saying good-bye to Al gets me thinking how much fun this trip was, how Eric, Hillary, Al, and I got along so well, how they never treated me like a little kid, and how much I loved Nepal and the Sherpas. Just two days ago, Jabion put a head strap on me and a pack load. I staggered for about a hundred yards before I had to give it back to a laughing Kami, who weighs about fifty pounds less than I. And that night, after we paid the Sherpas, I got up to go to the bathroom and there they were, at three A.M., gambling all their hard-earned money at cards.

How will I ever sit still in school now? What kid my age can I even tell about the wonderful feeling of standing on Yala Peak, with the blood rushing through me, the wind tearing at my eyes, the whole world of mountains out there in front of me to climb?

Al is now telling me about following a woman up a fixed rope on Everest, glad he decided to stay behind her because she looked so good in spandex, because if he had passed her, he would have been in the path of an avalanche. Then about another time, when his oxygen line froze up at 27,000 feet. And the deep, ever-changing crevasses on the Khumbu Icefall.

As Al talks and the traffic rushes by, I recall seeing Everest from Yala, the long scarf of windblown snow trailing off its summit, and now I can imagine a tiny dot of a figure standing there, waving a summit flag down at me. I look closer and closer and realize it is me waving that flag. I know now someday it will be.

"Got your tickets?" Al breaks me out of my thoughts.

"Yep. Right here."

We shake hands and I get in the van, ready for a trip harder, it seems, than Everest—finding my way home.

bigger ideas

*B*y now I'm an airport pro. It's Sunday morning and I'm on a plane to Miami, from there to Lima, Peru. But just last Friday night at midnight, I got off a plane, coming in from Wyoming.

Take twelve fourteen- and fifteen-year-olds, give them four instructors, and turn them loose in the wilds of Bighorn country in Wyoming for a month. Of course, you give them adequate supplies, but you make it challenging with summer snows, lightning storms, 10,000-foot peaks, unmarked trails, and sleeping out every night, no matter how wet, under a tarp. That's what National Outdoor Leadership School does.

Or at least part of what NOLS does. In the process, you learn all kinds of skills: trail cooking (yes, I can make cinnamon buns over a fire, or at least something resembling cinnamon buns), orienteering (finding your way around with only a compass and a map), first aid (I gave a lecture on hypothermia), and living in the wilderness.

Wyoming—Riverton, to be exact—is the home base of the Na-

tional Outdoor Leadership School, and I had made arrangements almost a year ago to go to a NOLS program. After my experiences at
URI's wilderness program, I knew I wanted to learn more outdoor
skills, so I signed up, never knowing I'd already have been to Nepal
before I got there. Yet all the experiences that Al gave me on the
trek didn't compare to what we did at NOLS.

What NOLS does most is teach you stuff you probably already
should know, and some people, even at NOLS, never learn. Like
sharing food. We had computerized rations. All our food for the
month was figured out by computer. We had to pack it all the first
day. Bags and bags of dried potatoes, rice, pasta, sugar, hummus,
candy, tea, coffee—all rationed out by computer. That meant we had
only so much at any one time. And it all had to be shared. Which
most did. Except for some guys, who would go off by themselves to
eat after they took an unusually big helping.

Leadership (in the title, I know) is another quality you learn.
Each day we had a new leader. That meant we all had the opportunity to make lots of decisions about routes we'd try, break times,
campsites, getting the group to cooperate, and, especially, decisions
about safety. One day I was leader, and my group of five climbed a
snow ridge about 5,000 feet up. From the bottom, I noticed a cornice
of snow hanging off, like snow on the edge of a roof. It looked pretty
dangerous, and I made a mental note to avoid it. Once we got to the
top, we were caught up in the view and didn't notice how close we
were getting to the cornice. We were not anywhere near the edge,
but I suddenly realized we were walking on nothing more solid than
15 feet of snow and ice, which could break off anytime. And I was
the leader! As calmly as I could, I tried to convince the group that
we had a problem and got everyone to walk gently back to the middle of the ridge where we were safe.

Some guys just didn't want to have to make decisions like that, and if, for example, we had a leader who hesitated with lightning and hail bouncing all around us, we would have been as bad off as walking out onto a snow cornice. I found out that I love being leader. Not just telling people what to do, but organizing and helping the group figure out how to do what it sets out to do in the best way possible.

I became good friends with guys like Aaron, a fifteen-year-old, red-haired, skinny kid who liked to climb as much as I did. Sterling, a wiry, quiet, Native American guy from Colorado, became another good friend because he was like Aaron and me, always game for more adventure, more climbing. The group got used to our getting back to camp after dark, because we'd always find a new peak to climb, even with our seventy-pound packs. And Eleanor with the cheerful smile. Most girls probably would not have wanted to be the only girl in the group. It didn't bother her at all. With her long brown hair and braces, Eleanor didn't look very tough, but she was much more strong-willed than most of the guys. She just laughed at all the practical jokes and stupid adolescent male stuff.

NOLS was very hard on some. After a ten-mile hike in the rain, or a shivering night under a soaking-wet tarp, a few people would want to leave and go home, but they always pushed themselves to stay. The group would encourage them and they stuck it out, every one of them, and they were happy in the end. All in all, it was fun to be with kids my own age like that, learning what I needed to know.

Which brings me to explaining my being on this plane to Lima, Peru. I had called Thor Keiser, one of the guys I had read about in ads in climbing magazines. He told me about all the trips his company, Condor Adventures, organizes to Ecuador, Argentina, Chile, and Peru, all with many challenging peaks, and not anywhere as expensive as Nepal. The line that got to me was "We can get you on some very high mountains that could be good training for the Himalayas, if you ever think about that."

I never told a soul about it, but one day in school, I began to think of Peru as a way to Mount Everest. I was sitting in English class, and we were doing dangling participles or something, and I started thinking about Nepal, about Everest. I could hardly sit still because everything was so vivid: the Everest summit, the smiling Sherpas, the heavy pull of my leg and back muscles up a steep stretch, and the sudden burst of early-morning light flooding down the mountain, all crowding into my head at once. I had to go to Everest!

I knew all about the altitude sickness, and the Khumbu Icefall, and the deaths, and the failure rate, and the expense, and the time. I also knew no one younger than seventeen had ever summited, but, corny as it sounds, everything came into focus for me. I know myself, and when I set my mind to something, I go ahead with it. That's why I'm on this plane to Lima. It's my first step to Everest.

My mother was working—the best time to get her next to late at night. She was looking at the computer screen, focused. I asked her if I could go to Peru to climb Huascarán. "All right, whatever." She waved me away, hardly aware. Dad was more alert. "Great idea! How are you paying for it?" That started a discussion that lasted for some time, because they realized going to Peru meant training for bigger climbs, but they agreed to support the trip, and I agreed to take out the garbage for life! Seriously, I had to agree to keep my grades up, otherwise all extracurricular activities were off. Climbing in Peru qualifies as an extracurricular activity.

Everest is still a small, secret shadow in my future, but it's real. Going to Nepal was like opening the door to the world. Now I have to learn to climb to its roof.

high altitude

JULY 27, 1994

Climbing the big mountains is very difficult, hard work, but, it is, first of all, inconvenient. In the United States, we're used to driving up to a paved parking lot and jumping out and getting into the "wilderness." For most of the world, "wilderness" doesn't have quotation marks around it. You have to work hard at just getting there. In my seventh-grade world history class, we learned that in the Middle Ages people used to go on pilgrimages to holy places to pray so they could get closer to heaven. All kinds of people would travel long distances together to these holy places, looking for spiritual peace. That's what climbing the big mountains is like—a pilgrimage. You first seek out the mountains; go a long distance by plane, helicopter, or bus; and, finally, when you see the holy place—the mountain—far in the distance, you have a long two-week hike to Base Camp. Then, gradually, as you climb the mountain, you get closer to heaven. Maybe that's why the Nepali have special religious ceremonies, and the Peruvian Indians pray, and the Tibetans chant—because the climbers of the big mountains get closer to God.

Anyway, that's what Peru feels like to me. A pilgrimage. I come here to see if I can start to think seriously about the biggest pilgrimage of all: Mount Everest, the tip of earth closest to heaven. How will I respond to high altitude? Will the very size of the mountains overwhelm me so much I get scared? What about glacier climbing? Bad weather? None of these questions really worry me. I'm very calm because inside I know this is what I'm supposed to be doing. I want to learn so that I can climb and look up to heaven from the highest place on earth.

If you took a large mall, sliced off its roof, and mixed all the stores together so that you have clothes hanging near sides of fly-covered beef, next to fresh produce, next to newspapers and books, next to cases of Coca-Cola and Inka-Cola (icky, sweet yellow soda), next to portable radios and Walkmen, and throw in lots of shoppers to mill around, then you'd have the streets of Lima. And getting through Lima's airport was even worse than Kathmandu's: it was dirtier, louder, and more confusing, with little Indian kids grabbing at your arms, yelling out for candy. *"Caramelo! Caramelo!"* They must take all the stuff down every night. I wonder where they store it, what they do about rain or snow and shoplifters, and all those little kids begging for *caramelos*.

I am walking through the outdoor market with Javier, Thor's business partner and my guide for our small climbing expedition. *Leader* is probably a better word than guide. A leader, especially on an expedition to South America, arranges all the logistics—food, equipment, transportation, schedules, and local help. He must also be a strong climber and be familiar with the mountain's routes and make necessary decisions. Javier is about five feet seven and all of 130 pounds. But he's very energetic, very lively. He is a native of

South America, speaks perfect Spanish (and English), and, because his face mirrors every emotion he feels, I can almost tell what he's saying to the Peruvians.

AUGUST 2, 1994

The crevasse, a split in the glacier, is no more than three feet wide. It's plenty deep, maybe 300 feet, but not very wide. I should be able to jump it—under ordinary circumstances. Which these are not. Javier and I are on the descent from Pisco, a 19,000-foot peak we're using as a warm-up for Huascarán. We are dog tired, because this was summit day. Up at three, climbing with crampons and roped in to each other, clawing our way to the summit, where I stood, head pounding in the thin air, on my highest peak ever. We came down quickly, stopping at Camp Two for our gear, to drink more water. Now it's getting late in the afternoon on the way to Camp One; Javier's behind me, ready to pull on the rope if I should slip on the glacier; and I'm looking for the only signs of our route up: the little holes in the snow made by our crampons.

On the ascent, the crevasse had been a challenge, but manageable, because we had only to jump across and land down about 2.5 or 3 feet below the lip we jumped from. Now, as tired as we are, we must jump the crevasse and, of course, land 3 feet higher. To make matters worse, Javier reminds me that you can't always trust the edge of a crevasse. The surface might look safe, but the crevasse could angle away underneath, and when you spring off the edge, it could crumble. You just don't know.

Javier puts me on belay, anchors into the ice, and waits as I get ready to jump. I'm breathing hard because of the altitude, because I'm excited, because I'm scared. I thrust forward and up, get one leg over the lip, kick the other foot's crampon point into the crevasse wall, sink my ice ax into the top, and pull myself up and over, all in one smooth move. OK, maybe it's not so smooth, maybe I struggle a bit, but I make it. I don't look down into the crevasse; I don't panic. I concentrate on what I must do, focus on getting across, and force my tired legs to spring. I anchor the rope into the ice, and Javier throws me our backpacks, and I put him on belay while he jumps across. We continue down as quickly as we can—speeding to safety, as Javier calls it—to get off the glacier before the sun melts more danger. (On the way up, we talked with a search team of four who were looking for a climber. The man hadn't been seen since early the previous day, and the search team thought he might have fallen into a crevasse. They asked us to keep an eye out for him.)

Jumping the crevasse takes only about ninety seconds, if that, but jumping the crevasse tells me a lot about this climbing business. You are in a tough situation, with little time to think, but must figure out a way to act patiently, correctly, while you ignore your whining body, which always wants the easy way. You do that not once or twice a week, or even once or twice a day, but sometimes four or five times a day, four or five times an hour. No one puts you in the tough situation but yourself, and you just love being there.

I'm not sure why, really. Kind of like the mixed feelings of coming down Pisco in the afternoon light. I want to go slowly because I have a pounding, violent headache, am dehydrated, and my knees are so stiff and tired I can hardly move. At the same time I want to hurry to hot food and a dry, warm place to sleep. I don't feel much like a pilgrim right now.

After a restless night at Advanced Base Camp (and a dinner of oatmeal), we stumble down to Base Camp, where we shiver in our heavy down jackets in 70-degree weather while everyone else walks around in T-shirts. Why are we so cold? At 17,000 feet, a person burns as many calories sitting still as a person uses exercising at sea level. Javier and I had been huffing and puffing our way to the summit of Pisco, using up every bit of heat-producing calories in our bodies. Think of how many we had burned up! After eating a big meal and resting, we are able to take off our jackets and walk around in the sun to warm up.

While we are walking around the little village near Base Camp, one scene repeats itself many times. Javier meets a villager, usually an older person, talks rapidly in Spanish, points to Pisco, then smiles and points to me. Then they look back at me, and after a while they start to smile and nod their heads as if they approve of what Javier said. I finally ask him what's going on.

"I'm asking them who was the youngest to summit Pisco. They don't know. So I ask them if any fourteen-year-olds ever did it. They say no. Maybe eighteen, maybe seventeen. Looks like you are the youngest by far."

I'm stunned. I never set out looking for a record for Pisco. That's not my purpose for coming here. Climbing is my purpose. Love of the mountains is my purpose. Pilgrimage. I have to admit, though, records can't hurt. Records can give you a big boost. I look up at Pisco's peak so far above us pointing at the sky, and I suddenly feel very strong. No one my age has ever been up there but me!

And just as quickly, I'm brought back to earth when one of the search party from the day before tells Javier that the climber died. They found him in the morning. Strangely, he had his passport and visa with him. Then the man tells Javier that six others had died on a nearby peak. Two fell into crevasses and four on a roped team fell together. About the same time I was standing on the summit of Pisco, feeling my heart pump in triumph, seven other hearts stopped forever. These climbers were doing exactly what I was doing. Well, almost exactly. Could I have died? Been one of them? I don't think so. I really don't. I'm too careful. Even when I jumped the crevasse, I knew I'd be OK. Even climbing up the steep part of the glacier, I knew I'd make it. It was hard; I got tired; but I knew I'd get to the top, knew I'd get down. The seven deaths have little impact on me. Maybe because I don't see the frozen, mangled bodies, or know any of them or their families. The seven deaths are almost bad rumors that I can forget about, erase from my mind so I can concentrate on Huascarán, over 3,000 feet higher than Pisco.

AUGUST 4, 1994

Butthead is the name I have for him, the only way I can think of him—the first person I meet in my all my climbing travels so far that I truly can't stand, who's really a self-centered jerk of the worst kind. After Pisco, Javier and I go to Huaraz where we are to meet a new member of our group—John, I'll call him—for our trip to Huascarán. As it turns out, I am to share a hotel room with him, and that's where the trouble begins. When I get there, his stuff is all over the room. Javier and I finally meet him when we are having dinner. John sits down with us, typical mountain guy with beard and well-worn clothes and boots. Next to us, by the way, are two American women quietly having dinner. John, after about five minutes of conversation, starts to laugh and says, loud enough for the two women to hear, "Did you guys hear about that cuckoo clock who went up with his passport and documents and died up there?"

"Excuse me, that was my husband." The American woman is glaring at John. "And her father."

Butthead doesn't say a word. Just sits there. No apologies; nothing. We all sit in embarrassed, tense silence until he abruptly gets up and just walks out. Javier and I apologize to the two women, say how badly we feel about the man's death, finish eating as quickly as we can and leave. I sneak a few looks at the mother and daughter and see the stunned look of horror on their faces, the uneaten food before them, and I realize that the seven mountain deaths are not mere rumors I can dismiss.

Outside, Butthead is waiting for us, smiling as if nothing had just happened. He wants us to go to a dance club with him. Javier and I say no, needing sleep for one thing, not interested for another.

My needing sleep doesn't bother Butthead. About one A.M., he pounds on the door, complaining loudly that the hotel owner won't let him bring someone he'd just met into the hotel. He wakes me out of a sound sleep. But he doesn't care. Same as the comments about the guy who died. I'm wide awake now, so mad I want to punch his stupid face. Then I realize I have to live and climb with this guy for two weeks.

AUGUST 5, 1994

A long day—much of it a never-ending wait in a town called Musho. For permits? For supplies? For our bus? We are not sure what the holdup is. Javier and I talk, walk around, ignore Butthead, who spends his time chewing tobacco. We eventually start our hike through beautiful eucalyptus forests, up a long ridge of open sky, closer to the 14,000-foot-high Base Camp. We stop for lunch: a can of sardines, bread, a banana, and warm water—ugh! (We have sardines often because they are easy to pack, but they're so full of oil, so heavy, I don't care if I ever see one again.) The high-mountain Base Camp experience is almost always the same, no matter where it is. You have to sit around a lot. Actually your body is acclimatizing, getting used to the new demands higher altitudes put on it. The higher you go, the thinner the air. Kind of like whole milk and skim milk. If you're used to drinking whole milk, then skim milk's going to taste awful, almost like water. It takes getting used to. The same for air. The thinner the air, the less oxygen it has. If your body is used to sea-level air, it takes a while to get used to the thin air up high. If you're too active when you first get to higher elevations, you'll get headaches and gradually get pretty sick to your stomach. If you acclimatize well, slowly enough to adjust but not so slowly you are bored to death, you can keep moving up to higher and higher elevations, each time adjusting, each time allowing for the adjustment, always keeping an eye on your activity and how your body handles what you do. Otherwise, the altitude will get you every time.

Inez, our cook, speaks little English, but she has a Spanish-English dictionary, which I try to use hanging around Base Camp. César, a local guide who will climb with us, laughs at my terrible Spanish pronunciation, but so what, I'm learning. Base Camp always teaches me patience. I can see the huge Huascarán before me, feel its late-afternoon shadow, and my body's like a little puppy that wants to go out and play, that can't wait to run up the glacier, to get to the top. Javier and Inez are there to slow me down, and I sit around listening to them, and sit around some more reading the Spanish-English dictionary.

AUGUST 6, 1994

To Camp One. Up huge slabs of slanted rock in the double boots we have to wear that are so stiff it's like picking your way up steep concrete in ski boots, carrying a heavy pack. Camp One. Sounds like a place already set up. Sounds as if it has tents and maybe a wooden fence and a sign that reads "Camp One." It's really a place on the glacier that is approximately near where past climbers may have set up their camps. In this case, there is no sign at all of any previous camps. The glacier moves in such a way that what was probably flat before is quite steep now. So we have to invent Camp One. That means making snow platforms for tents: digging out and packing down an area big enough for a tent, small enough to protect the tent from wind. Funny feeling, to be shoveling snow in the cold wind, 17,000 feet up a glacier, then curling up in my sleeping bag with sunscreen, food, water, boots, glasses next to me so they won't freeze. As I try to sleep, chattering away in my heavy down clothes, in a thick sleeping bag in an unheated tent on a glacier high up on the highest mountain in Peru, I start to think: this is my summer vacation, and every kid I know is at the beach surfing!

AUGUST 7, 1994

Now comes the hard part. The steep section of ice. You have to dig in the edges of your crampons and climb at an angle. Our party of Javier, Butthead, César, me, and two helpers is struggling up the steep ice, loaded down with all our equipment for Camp Two, when we come to an overhanging ice cliff. César and Javier climb up, anchor two ropes into the ice, and we jumar up—that is, we have a rope for each hand and work our way up with two little hand devices. First, you slide one jumar up and squeeze it into the rope for a good grip, then you alternate with the other jumar in the hand, all the way up. All the way up in this case is not very far—12 feet.

Try this: Put a ladder against a building or house fairly close to the wall. Start climbing the ladder from the *underside*. Now pretend the ladder's made of ice. And you're going to have to climb it by pulling yourself up with those jumar devices, with all your weight on your hands, and kicking your crampons into the ice for balance. Now the best part: Imagine that ladder is at 18,000 feet, where you can't help but see far below you the white and blue of glacier, the green landscape, and the tiny dots of roofs of a distant village, and you know that five guys are waiting to see if you'll chicken out.

Can you do it? Of course you can. You have to!

Everybody does make it. Even Butthead—his special way. He has to keep his pack on to show the rest of us weaklings how a man climbs. Naturally, he has a hard time, almost toppling backward, gasping for breath in the thin air. We weaklings pull our packs up on ropes and just laugh at Butthead's efforts to prove his manhood.

Now we're on a long spine of a ridge up to Camp Two. In beautiful sunshine, we pass huge sculptured icefalls, then make camp, cutting out snow platforms again, melting snow to drink (you have to drink seven, eight quarts a day just to keep hydrated at this altitude), cooking on the glacier, doing all the stuff the famous climbers do! And I'm at 20,000 feet, higher than I've ever been before, higher than some planes cruise. I do have a slight headache, and any physical effort makes me breathe as hard as if I were running, but overall I'm doing fine! I'm making it!

AUGUST 8, 1994

Summit Day. Up at four. I put on three layers of clothes. Everyone else is packing. I'm still getting dressed. Wearing too much? I'm not sure. Javier's in a hurry. "Come on. Let's get this going." I don't have mittens on, just gloves. Hands numb in dark cold. We get up steep sections in the dark. I have to stop, get mittens out of pack. Javier has to warm my hands. We do switchbacks over crevasses. Javier and I are roped together, then Butthead and César. Each pair determines its own route by strength and terrain. Our headlamps pick up helpful signs: bamboo sticks with red flags laid out by previous climbers. The ice is light blue as dark weakens to dawn. Then *wham!* The edge of the sun jumps over a peak and its rays hit your face. More sunscreen. Warmer. Switchbacks and more switchbacks. After every one, I think: This is it. We're there. This has to be the highest point.

But it isn't. We keep climbing. Harder and harder to breathe. Same as at the end of a seven-mile run, when you push the last half mile and you're almost there and you want to force maximum effort. Only here you have farther to go. Another summit? No, just another peak almost as high. False summits, they're called. Legs dragging. Using sides of crampons, ski poles, ice axes. Javier's tired; everyone's dragging. I look at Butthead, gasping like the rest of us, and think what he said to me last night in Camp Two. "Heard you're thinking of Everest. You think you can just take a NOLS course, come here, and then go to Everest?" Then he laughed his sarcastic laugh and turned over in his sleeping bag, leaving me more motivated than ever to summit. We climb forty minutes and rest five. Forty more and rest five more. Each time we seem close, the mountain gods laugh at us: No, that is not the summit, you still have a way to go.

And then we are here—22,205 feet above sea level. The highest place in Peru. For some reason, I don't hurt anymore. My breathing feels normal. I'm too tired for great exhilaration, but I shout out and hug Javier. We break out summit flags, take photos, pee on the summit. (Lots of guys pee on every summit they reach. Like leaving your scent. Of course, there's the danger of frostbite, which I don't even want to think about.) Unlike at Pisco, this time I know I'm the youngest ever to summit Huascarán, and I feel a rush of power surface through my fatigue. I look down at Cordillera Negra, a dirt mountain range in the distance, and want to say, bring it on, bring any of them on, I can climb them all!

We begin our descent just as it starts snowing. Javier puts me in front, which means I find the route, set the pace. I'm in charge! First time I have such a responsibility. Same as at Pisco: I want to hurry, to get down, to rest, eat, get warm; but I know better. We must be careful. A slip on the glacier has meant the death of many tired climbers. Soon snow covers the crampon holes, but I know I have us on the right track because I find the bamboo wands easily, and I lead us through the increasing snow to our Camp Two. We pack our equipment and keep going down the steep glacier to the cliff area.

At one point, I hear Javier behind me yell to Butthead, "Keep that ax in your uphill hand!" (Common and accepted practice among climbers to carry your ice ax in uphill hand. If you slip and you lean uphill as you fall, simply dig in your ax and you'll "self-arrest.") I turn to see Butthead, who waves his ax, in downhill hand, at Javier. "Don't worry," he says. "I didn't take a NOLS course. You don't have to pamper me." Butthead strikes again.

We rappel down the overhang. Getting close to the edge, I accidentally knock Javier's ski pole over, and it bounces down into a crevasse below. Javier explodes at me for my carelessness. I screwed up. I admit it, apologize, let his words go. We are in a dangerous place, and there's no time to analyze things; I have no explanations for Javier. We just climb down and keep going. In five minutes, we forget about the whole thing. All I want now is a strong anchor, a safe rappel, a safe descent to Camp One, where we can set up tents, eat oatmeal, and sleep.

AUGUST 9, 1994

I wake up with my face wet. Did I drool all night? No. My whole face is blistered: cheeks, forehead, even the roof of my mouth. I come out of my tent, and the looks from Javier and César make me feel like Frankenstein's monster. I had used sunscreen—SPF 50—but not enough of it, and I go the rest of the way down to Base Camp wearing the ugliest face on the mountain.

We slump into Base Camp, looking like war survivors, as usual. The camp has grown in the three days we were on the mountain—almost seventy people wanting to climb various routes up Huascarán, including a priest and twenty students who are going to climb and pray. Base Camp has become a little city, and all seventy citizens seem to be staring at my face as we make our way to our tents.

Inez smothers my face in ointment, and I lie around my tent reading the Spanish-American dictionary, keeping out of the sun, away from the stares. Inez makes a wonderful meal, which looks so good, but I can't eat it because of the sunburn on the roof of my mouth. I sit there anyway, in a circle with Javier, Butthead, César, and Inez. Butthead asks me to pass him the long thin salami that everyone but me is sharing. I have come across the Spanish word for penis, *pene*, in the dictionary, and can't resist the opportunity for a little revenge. I pass the salami to Butthead and say, without a trace of a smile, *"Pene."* To which he says, "Thank you." Everyone cracks up. Everyone except Butthead. Obviously, he knows no Spanish.

AUGUST 12, 1994

The record-setting young mountain climber, the newest celebrity-hero on the mountain-climbing scene, returns from his latest conquest in style. How? In the back of the bus, on the floor, next to the toilet, squished between cases of Coca-Cola, back twisted into his pack, lying there for eight hours unable to move or see out. It's the only space he could get.

Our bus tickets to Lima, reserved and paid for well in advance, have been resold—a common way to increase business, we find out. We refuse to get off the bus to Lima; the people occupying the seats we paid for will not move. What to do? We won't move; we keep the bus from leaving. An hour passes, all the other passengers scream at us. The driver, the one who sold our reserved tickets, finally does us a big favor: he lets us squeeze onto an already crowded bus. I end up on the floor, bouncing between the Coke bottles, the smell of the bathroom leaking out at me, my face still an ugly mass of blisters. All this is years away, it seems, from the summit of Huascarán. All part of the pilgrimage, I keep telling myself. All part of what I will do. And when the bus pulls into Lima in the gray light of dawn, and I unfold myself from the bottom of the bus, I feel so happy— stiff, sore, blistered, smelling, exhausted, but so happy to be where I am.

getting physical

So you want to climb Everest, I ask my body, and you think you can

do that? Then take this. And so I run the stairs. Hospital stairs. I run eight flights up. I run eight flights down, in my new shorts that are weighted with four-and-a-half pounds on each leg. For at least an hour. Three fast laps up and down, then an easier lap. Around ten o'clock, when no one uses the stairs, after my homework. No mountains to climb near the ocean, so I got permission to run the stairs of the highest building around—the Newport Hospital. Sometimes there'll be a guy watching me through the little window of the door to the eighth floor, like now. He's locked up in the mental observation floor, looks out, and sees me huffing and puffing up the stairs, get near his door and then turn around and run down, come back up gasping for breath, get close to his door, then run back down again, then a third, fourth, fifth, sixth time, gasping louder and louder, sweat drooling off my chin, looking more and more tired, still running. I look at him looking at me. He must wonder why he's locked in while there's this obviously disturbed person running up and down the stairs like a dog chasing his tail. He might report me to a nurse; she'd want to lock me up. Which she'd be sure to do if she saw me when I got home from running stairs, doing my five hundred sit-ups and my "uglies"—exercises in which I lie on my stomach and arch my back while lifting my legs.

Two weeks now. And I'm so tired I don't know if it's doing any good or not. But it is serious training. I talked to Thor Keiser in September; he has an expedition to Ecuador set up for me, said I need the experience, but also said he's sure I can do Everest if I train hard. I told him I signed up for a high-angle rescue and evaluation course in California, just so I know what to do in case of a mountain accident. Plus I'd taken an emergency medical technician course here in Rhode Island, even learning to stitch wounds on my own. Thor loved it. But he said I had to get more physical, too. So that's what I'm doing. Running stairs and sit-ups are only part of it, thanks to Nel Poisson.

Nel had read an article about me and called to see if I was interested in the vitamin products he represented. He asked about my training and said I really needed someone to kick my butt if I wanted to get into the condition I needed to be in. Then he smiled and said he'd be willing to do the kicking—which is exactly what he has done. He's a personal trainer who's trying to get his business going, and he hopes training me will give him some exposure.

We started two weeks ago—the Newport Athletic Club allowed Nel to use its facilities—and Nel wasted no time. He started me on 1,000-rep workouts immediately. I thought I was in good shape until Nel gave me fifty pounds and twenty-five leg extensions, twenty-five leg curls, twenty-five squats, twenty-five calf raises, then repeated the whole sequence four times—without stopping. I almost threw up. My head was spinning, lungs hurting, but I loved it, knew it was what I needed. On to the upper body. Finish with deep push-ups off a bar that really works your pecs. My whole body was shaking with fatigue that first day, that first week—even now. I'm almost finished with the second week, have increased the weights, included running the stairs, the sit-ups, and the uglies—these last my own ideas— and am still so tired I don't know how such a nice middle-aged guy like Nel can be so mean.

Doing push-ups yesterday, I kept saying to him, "I hate you!" in a joking manner, and he'd just smile and keep the count going. I'd get so shaky I'd want to quit, and he'd get another one out of me, then another, laughing at me snarling at him. Nel tells me to zone out the pain, so I imagine this beautiful girl—just like the girl two seats in front of me in math class, the one whose hair I study every day— across a canyon and a big gorilla is chasing her, and if I do three more push-ups I can rescue her, and she will run to me because I saved her. "Two more, Mark!" Nel rasps in my ear. The girl is screaming as the gorilla gets near her. She feels its stinking hot breath on her face. "One more! When you got nothing left, you still have one more!" The beautiful girl struggles to get away, and I, on my last push-up, burst through the jungle and grab her in my pumped-up arms and pull her away from the hot stinking breath of the gorilla.

"OK," Nel says. And I collapse onto the floor. No girl. Just trembly, shaky arms, gasps of breath, just another workout. Nel and I have a very good relationship.

Running stairs forces me to zone out the pain, to think about what I've been doing since Peru. First, it was up to Maine in August to hike with Frank Madeira. We climbed Mount Katahdin and camped in Baxter State Park, and Frank wanted to hear all about my trips. I told him what I had done in the eight months since I hiked with him: ice climbing, Nepal, NOLS, Peru. Then he told me about his hikes in the Alps and the northern New England mountains. We sat there for hours, just two guys, tired after a long day of hiking, talking at their campsite. It's hard to remember sometimes he's seventy-eight—sixty-four years older than me.

Talking with Frank made me realize how far I've come in eight months, how climbing has become my life. This is what happens when a thirteen-year-old jump-starts his adult life. Someone told me once about breaking through comfort zones, about pushing yourself to do things beyond what you are comfortable with. How if you stay inside your comfort zone, you never grow, like people who seldom leave the island I live on. They're comfortable there. I know I've already stretched my comfort zone. You could drop me off for a month in South America, Nepal, even Tibet, and I bet I'd survive OK. I wouldn't panic. I'd be in my comfort zone. I wouldn't even get home-sick.

Nothing's going to change at home, but as long as I have an opportunity to change my life, to do my life the way I want to do it, to make it as good as I want it to be, then I'm going for it. No matter how many reps it takes, no matter how many stairs I have to run, I'm going to do it. Every kid has the same chance—but too many of us think we have so much time ahead, we kill off the present. I see a lot of guys my age putting themselves into the future, always saying "Can't wait till I get my license," or "Can't wait till I get out of high school," or "Can't wait till I get away from home." The whole time they're idling like a car at a stoplight. Still using up gas, but stopped. Not going anywhere. They're stopping themselves, though, waiting till that someday; then when the light finally changes, they're not used to moving.

Not me. Just like running these stairs. Eight minutes to go for my hour. Legs getting tight, weak, sweat stinking up the stairwell, my mom's dinner rising up into my throat. But I'm still moving. I'm not waiting for my license or anything else.

I'm lucky because I acquire climbing skills very fast. I also have the pulmonary capacity, according to an expert I checked with. He asked me about my height (six feet one), weight (about 175), and basic dimensions, then he explained that my body size would give me the same capacity as a twenty-five-year-old man. So I'm getting ready. I could play football for the next three years, wander the halls of Middletown High, get my license, and maybe, just maybe, if I get enough courage, ask out a few girls. Or I can concentrate on climbing, carve out my own life, one rep at a time, one flight of stairs at a time, until I get to the top of Everest.

What I'll need most is experience. The kind of experience that climbers like Scott Fischer develop over the years in the mountains, experience that has taught him to deal with difficult situations with calm confidence. To get that experience I need to climb more. To climb, I need more money, more sponsors. That's another skill I should have told Frank about. I'm fourteen, but I've learned to pick up the phone, call equipment companies, tell them what I've done, where I'm going, what I need, and ask for their financial support.

It was hard at first. Just like doing these stairs. But after calling or writing letters for an hour every day, you get used to it. Even get used to people saying no. You can't let it bother you. You're not going to summit all the time on the mountains, either. So just make another call. I learned to be comfortable with going to a retail show, walking up to sponsors, and introducing myself. I also learned that lots of potential sponsors won't go near me because of my age—they don't want to be responsible if something goes wrong. Some just won't even listen. And others have been willing to sponsor a young kid no one's ever heard of before. They've given me equipment, sometimes money, always more opportunity to continue.

Three minutes to go. I'm staggering now, last lap, four more flights up, then down, then home, sit-ups, uglies, shower, bed. My father is waiting for me downstairs in the car, reading his magazine; my mother is at home. Most parents would look at their kid after he did one of these workouts and respond like the guy looking out the door on the eighth floor: their kid is crazy. Not my parents. They want me to run stairs. *Make* me. If I want to take a couple of days off, they're all over me. For good reason. They want only one thing from me: all-out commitment. The same commitment they wanted when I started climbing is what they insist on for Everest: the best equipment, the best instruction, and the best training.

They will not let me go unless all three are satisfactory. Do they push me? To work out, yes. So I'll be ready. That's the only pressure I get from them. To be as ready as I can be, because—as my father always says—the mountain is unforgiving. That's why he'll always drive me here, or wherever I have to go, to get ready. Preparation is always important to him. He was a cop for many quiet nights on the island of Jamestown, but he was always ready for those times it was anything but quiet. He taught me to take care of rifles and firearms when I was young so they are always safe in our house; taught me to have a clean, neat work area; taught me always to take care of equipment right away, and so many other things I forget what they are; they just became good habits.

Having the support of sponsors, family, friends, and particularly of my parents could turn to pressure because of expectations, I suppose, but that never happens to me. My parents want to see me have the opportunity to do what I want to do. They also want me to be well prepared. They'll even support my Everest goal as much as they can. I realize the price tag is high, and I have little sponsor money at this point, but I know that it will work out. I know my parents and sponsors will somehow come up with the money. My mother says she's lucky to be able to help me, that if Everest is meant to be, somehow or other the money will become available. To me, $1,000 is overwhelming; $24,000 is unthinkable. My parents worry about whether I'll be safe, whether there'll be a way to get me there, but they never once put any pressure on me to climb Everest. Only to be prepared in every way possible.

Finished with my workout, I walk out into the cold night air, drinking Coke, glad Nel can't see me. If he saw the Coke, I'd surely die the next workout. I must admit I resist what he says about diet. I eat a typical teenage diet: junk food and all. Can't help myself, it seems. The way I figure it is this: If I'm giving 1,000-rep workouts three days a week; stairs, uglies, and sit-ups every night; and a five- or six-mile run most days, I guess a few Twinkies or Big Macs or Ben & Jerry's ice cream won't make much difference.

ecuador: success and failure

NOVEMBER 28, 1994

I'm off to Ecuador. First, though, I have to go through my usual ritual with teachers. Most see the benefits in my travel, my climbs. Others see the kids coming in every day, working hard, while I get to go off and "play" in some adventurous place. They resent my coming to them to get my assignments ahead of the other kids. They grumble that I'm extra work for them and that my taking off isn't fair to the others.

I have only one answer for them: Mr. Krupowicz. He looks like what a science teacher should look like: tall, glasses, serious, patient, quiet. Now, he's no longer a science teacher but the assistant superintendent of schools, and he thinks what I'm doing is far more educational than sitting in a classroom and lets teachers know that. It's unusual to have an administrator like Mr. Krupowicz fight for your staying out of school, but he's making sure that all my teachers understand how much you can learn on a trip where you have to cope in a new language and deal with very different societies, food, customs, even geography. That's before you even get to a mountain. I've been to places most kids my age never even check out on a map.

I still have to keep up with my assignments. Sometimes I ask way ahead, so I can double up reading or math assignments before I leave. Most of the time, teachers give me my work the day I leave, like this time, so I have a briefcase full of books to lug around. Studying on a trip is the last thing I feel like doing, especially at the end of a hard climbing day. But that's the bargain I made: stay up with school, do the assignments, and be very thankful to Mr. Krupowicz.

When I land in Miami, I look for other team members. I've never met any of them, but they spot me first—maybe because I'm the only guy walking through Miami Airport with ski poles. And I recognize them, too. You can spot climbers easily. Say you're in a restaurant in Yosemite full of hikers and tourists. Two guys walk in, one's limping, both have dirty T-shirts, callused, cut hands covered in chalk, and they're talking about piano moves and beta on the wall. Climbers. We introduce ourselves. Gary dredges for gold in Alaska, Dean is a physicist, Tom is an ob-gyn doctor from Mississippi, Dave is an engineer of laser products, Louis is a lawyer from Connecticut, Greg is a fire jumper from Colorado. Javier and Luiz, from Colorado, are the expedition leaders. Gary says to me, "Hear we got some fourteen-year-old kid we're waiting for. He's pretty young for this stuff, don't you think?"

"Hey!" I blurt out. "That's me!"

They all stop talking and stare at me as if I were from another planet. "You're the fourteen-year-old?" Gary asks. "How'd you get out of school?"

I want to say the magic word—Krupowicz. But I just smile.

NOVEMBER 29, 1994

It's always fun to drive in foreign countries. The drivers are all speed demons, the roads to the mountains always muddy hairpin curves and long drop-offs, and you get to see a lot of the country whiz by the window. We're in two Toyota trucks, on the way to Pichincha, a 15,000-foot peak. We speed through humid, misty rain forest and finally get to our hut at 12,000 feet.

Louis and I, both coming from sea level, have pounding headaches, so much so we have to stay in the hut while the other guys, all of whom live at some altitude, climb easily. Louis and I talk about flying into Quito, Ecuador's major city, last night, and how weird the lights seemed to be, as if you're flying deeper and deeper into an abyss. Quito is, at 9,000 feet, built into the side of a mountain, so you see hillside lights all the way down. The airport and the city were like Kathmandu: dirty, hot, fumes and noise, all stuff I'm used to by now.

NOVEMBER 30, 1994

I'm getting to know just how crazy our driver, Juan Carlos, really is. We're heading for Cayambe, our next peak. We're speeding, as usual, up the side of some mountain road. Below us are green, tropical hillsides, and terracing like in Nepal. Off in the distance, peaks pop up through the clouds. A wonderful, warm place to be on November 30. We're tooling along when we hit a section of mud, and the truck begins to spin. On one side there is sheer cliff, on the other, a 400-foot drop, toward which the truck slides sideways. I'm on the cliff side and see the edge get closer and closer. I'm yelling "Look at this! Look at this!" but the other guys are all white knuckles and hanging on, their eyes closed. The truck slides to a stop inches from the edge. We all pile out the other side and watch Juan

Carlos as he slowly, carefully backs the truck away from the cliff. For some reason, we decide to walk through the rest of the muddy section of road, legs a little weak, hearts still thumping.

On Cayambe, we practice for our summit bid the next day by learning how to use ropes. You always use ropes as climbers, but you're not always roped together in such large teams. I've never before been on a team of four and I learn how much the word *teamwork* really means, especially on the hard ice of a glacier, which much of Cayambe is. Everyone must be aware of the climbing pace of each of the others and concentrate to stay synchronized. It's a little like those three-legged races or a drill team. You have to be very careful to keep your footsteps coordinated. Of course, if one person slips on the ice, then the others can arrest, or stop, his fall, unless the whole team is in a truck and is sliding through the mud toward a 400-foot cliff.

DECEMBER 1, 1994

We're up at three A.M., get to the glacier, rope up, and we're off. Dawn finds us far up the glacier. Louis and I are, however, soon wasted; the pace is much too fast for us on the first days at altitude. Besides, another group came into the hut last night, and, even though we asked them to keep the noise down, their loud talk kept me awake. Two hours' sleep, no acclimatizing . . .

I'm falling asleep on every break. It gets to Louis so much that Luiz has to help him get down to the hut. That means we have six on a rope. (Sounds like a good name for a band.) Which means another type of dance. We get to about 18,000 feet, and three of the team go for the last 996 feet to the summit while three of us wait in the snow. They're back a half hour later. Too much snow. They can't fight their way through the deep powder to make it to the summit.

Back at the hut, we're all a little frustrated, but not much. No

one summited, but Louis feels better. The other guys are pleased
with getting to 18,000, and I need the acclimatizing. Later, the
group that had so much fun late last night comes to us. "Hey. We're
going for the summit early tomorrow. You guys wanna keep it down
tonight?" Yeah. Sure. Right.

DECEMBER 3, 1994

Next stop: Cotopaxi, the world's third-highest active volcano and
Ecuador's highest peak. When I returned from Peru, my plane flew
right over the mouth of its crater, and I could look right down inside.
From the plane, it looked like a huge, round sugar doughnut. And
here I am about to climb it. Juan Carlos and I bounce along in our
red truck to Cotopaxi Base Camp. I like the sense of adventure Juan
Carlos brings to every ride. We're flying by little shops with big hog
carcasses hanging down, past an old, dead bus at a crazy angle on
the side of the road. Then out into the country. I look at the
speedometer: 120! Much too fast—even for Juan Carlos! Then I
realize it's *kilometers*, not *miles*, per hour. Nothing stops Juan Carlos.
He loves the challenge of a difficult route as much as any climber.
We get closer to Base Camp. The trail—no longer a road—is a
steep, 45-degree angle, all slippery mud and sand. Stubborn Juan
Carlos keeps bouncing us along, wheels churning, motor whining,
until he almost rolls the truck over. Only then does he finally stop.
We get out to wait for the other guys. Funny that I'm the only one
with Juan Carlos. Everyone else has crowded into the other truck. I
wonder why?

The Cotopaxi Base Camp is at least a mile up a very steep trail,
and we have to carry everything there ourselves. Great workout for
the legs: sixty pounds of backpack and equipment on a long uphill.
Especially if you also have to carry a briefcase full of schoolbooks!

Picture it: A group of climbers struggle with heavy packs as they hike up the steep trail in the mist of the wilds of Ecuador. One has the same double load as the others, but in his right hand he carries a briefcase. Make sure you get that homework done. No excuses. I feel like a little kid with a lunch box!

DECEMBER 5, 1994

By four A.M., we're well on our way, climbing by headlamps. We've already lost Luiz. Five minutes into the climb he had to quit, stomach was killing him. Must be giardia, a germ known as beaver fever because beavers leave it in streams, and when people drink what looks like clear mountain water, they pick it up. That's why we drink our water with iodine. It tastes lousy, but it's clean.

As the light grows stronger, we see another team ascending near us. Javier, the competitor that he is, gets into a kind of race with them, pushing us to go faster. We're roped together and making solid progress: we want to be at the summit by eight, before melting can cause problems on the glacier. Javier picks up the pace. It's clear he wants to get to the summit before those other guys. We can see the summit by now, far up in the gold light of early morning, and we follow Javier's fast pace, wanting to stand on that crater.

After a half hour of heart-pounding, nonstop climbing, Louis pleads with us to slow down, and Javier slows the pace, watching the other team move ahead. Louis has a real altitude problem—something you don't know about until you get up high. Some climbers can train like crazy at lower altitude but just can't perform well at heights. Others just get into it easily. It's a risk every altitude climber takes, and it looks like Louis is one of the unlucky ones.

About 200 feet from the summit, Louis yells out, "Gotta stop.

I'm hallucinating. Can't go on." Javier pulls him aside, digs a hole in the snow, and says, "Stay here. Whatever you do, don't move!" Louis sits down, doubled over with exhaustion, and we continue to the summit. Soon I'm on my first summit in Ecuador (19,347 feet), another big step on my pilgrimage to Everest, the youngest ever to stand on the flat top of the crater of the world's third-highest active volcano. Well, not very active for about twenty years maybe, but you can still smell the sulfur. I can look off and see other peaks poking through the clouds below us, then turn around and look far down into the dark mouth of the volcano. What do I do at this exciting moment? I fall asleep, that's what I do. We had gone to bed at nine last night. Which is good. We got up two hours later to leave for the summit. Which is bad. Two hours is not enough sleep for me. The summit is sunny, not too cold, and it feels so good to just stretch out while the other guys take pictures, kind of fun to be hanging out on top of a mountain that looks just like a little kid's drawing of a volcano. Before I know it, Gary's waking me up. Time to rope up, get Louis, and head down.

Louis, however, is not there. We can see far down the steep slope, but Louis is nowhere in sight. Javier's face tells his thoughts: If he fell, it's my fault. Should never have left him—not experienced enough. The lower we go, the more nervous we get. Still no Louis. Finally we come around a bend, and there, sitting on a rock in the sun, a fully recovered Louis greets us with a smile. Javier practically hugs him.

We take the downhill express: we take our crampons off and glissade, or slide, down the steep snow slope. Javier skies—on his boots. We whoop and holler like little kids out sledding on a snow day off from school. Momentum carries us close to a rock field, and we self-arrest with our ice axes, laughing at the danger we avoid. Soon we are down at the hut, sweating in the afternoon sun, ready for a long afternoon nap. What a wonderful way to spend a December day in Ecuador.

DECEMBER 7, 1994

I wonder how often this happens: a summit bid stopped by a strike and a riot. We're on our way to Chimborazo, the highest peak in Ecuador, only to be told that the road is closed. Up ahead, there is a strike of government workers that's turned into a riot. It's so bad that cars and trucks coming down the road take the chance of being turned over, set afire. Not us. We turn back, stay at a small hotel, surrounded by armed guards, check out the local outdoor market, and check Chimborazo off our to-do list.

DECEMBER 8, 1994

We go to Illiniza instead. At 17,394 feet, it's not the highest, but it's certainly a more technically demanding climb, which means that you have to be able to use a lot of equipment like rope and pitons—things you stick into rocks to hold the ropes—to get to the top. Juan Carlos stops the truck on the road, points to a trail, smiles, and tells us it's only about nine miles to the Base Camp hut. I hoist on my backpack (50 pounds), grab my briefcase (150 pounds, at least), and head up the steep trail.

We've lost two members by now. Tom, the ob-gyn doctor, was called home because his partner had a heart attack. Tom was so mad he said he was going to bring the guy three Big Macs with extra cheese. Just as well he's leaving. He's a specialist in sex-change operations, and he made me nervous. Always wondered if I'd wake up one morning feeling a little funny. Louis has had enough. He's done. He tried very hard, but the altitude just did him in.

We hike through foggy mist and finally get to the hut at dark to find a lock on the door, which an ice ax quickly takes care of. An ice ax cannot take care of the weather, though. We're pretty high in altitude, but so near the equator that fog, mist, and rain are as common as snow.

DECEMBER 9, 1994

The fog is so thick that we cannot find a route to climb Illiniza, second day in a row. It's frustrating to know the mountain is so close; you've come all this way to climb it, but you can't climb what you can't see. So we head back to Quito. It's frustrating, that's all you can say about it. On the way back to Quito in the rain, I think about how the Red Sox must feel after losing four out of five on a West Coast road trip. All that way just to lose four games. All this way and not climb. Nobody else is very upset. The other guys are happy with the other climbs, with having done well at altitude, and look forward to going home. Not me. I'm not satisfied with the other climbs, and I'm not ready to go home yet, either.

DECEMBER 11, 1994

While the other guys head for the airport, Javier and I are on our way back to Cayambe, where we've chosen a new route to try. We get back to the same hut we used before and get soaked in the rain that seems to have followed us all the way from Quito. We patiently wait out the afternoon gloom playing cards, reading, looking out at the rain. And all it does is drip. All night. We wake to the same dripping sound, the same foggy gloom, the same hanging out. Then a couple of hours later it stops, allowing us to try to get up a new back-ridge route that's full of crevasses and challenging glacier climbing.

It's now near dark, it's raining again, we're still on the mountain. We can hear avalanches growling like distant dragons, ready to attack us at any minute. Javier and I dig a snowcave and try to start our little stove, ready to spend the night at least safe, if not dry. Soon it's pitch dark, and the snowcave drips freezing water on our heads, and the stove won't start. Javier looks around and says, "We better get out of here." And we do. Stuff our gear into bags, put on harnesses with numbed, wet hands, start down the trail, and don't stop until we are inside the hut, where dragon avalanches can't get us.

DECEMBER 14, 1994

Still raining. Two days later. More cards. More drips. I left my brief-case in Quito, so I can't even do homework. Finally, in the afternoon, soaked and defeated, we hike down to meet Juan Carlos in his truck. Four days of rain. On the way back to Quito, I realize I've been on a roll since I was thirteen. Never an injury, not the least hint of a setback; I've been spoiled by success. I became so used to hitting every target I aimed at, I forgot what Thor told me once: you just don't always summit. In fact, get used to failing, because it's going to happen a lot more than the successes. Each failure to summit is another step, and each step is a victory in learning weather conditions, and the beauty of a mountain, and working with people.

When I get out of the truck in Quito, I'm so wet I squish when I walk. One for six. That's my Ecuador scorecard. Stopped by headaches, snow, fog, a riot, rain, and more rain. But you won't hear me complain or whine about bad luck. At least not around climbers. No matter how much time and money the trip has cost, no matter what fatigue and discomfort you've put up with, you learn you just don't always summit. You accept failure as part of the mountain.

CHAPTER EIGHT

argentina

The climbing team assembled here, in Thor Keiser's living room in Denver, is auditioning for Mount Everest. Here's how it works: As owner of Condor Adventures, Thor gets the word out through ads in magazines and word of mouth that he's planning an expedition in South America, as training for Everest. People contact him. Some he's known from the past; others have heard about him; others, like me, answer his ad. We all send our climbing résumés, and Thor responds with an invitation or refusal to join his commercial expedition (which means we pay him to lead us).

Later today, we'll head for Ten-Mile Canyon to practice jumar techniques, which will be like tryouts for the basketball team. Out there, Thor will determine whom he needs to watch closely, or who may have exaggerated his ability on his résumé and will be told to go home. But now Thor's checking out our gear, and I'm checking out my new teammates. First, there's the over-the-hill guys like Pat Caffrey, a middle-aged, overweight lumberjack from Montana; and

Tony Tonsing, another out-of-shape climber, who saw this training as a waste of time because, after all, he's already climbed Gasherbrum II in Pakistan; and Carlo Rocca, a sixty-three-year-old bypass survivor. Then there are the able climbers like tall George Fuller, a very good climber who's helped Thor in the past. I should also mention Kat (Katarina Straskraba), Thor's girlfriend, a good climber and skier; and Javier, whom I climbed with in Peru and Ecuador.

Funny what people fate brings together. Most kids my age get into certain classes, or on a team, or somehow get to be friends and stick together, at least for a season or a school year. Peer groups. Friends. Climbing doesn't let that happen. It brings all kinds of people together: the leaders, the ones who sign up, the ones who are invited, and it puts them all in very close situations, sometimes life-or-death situations. Then a week later, you're in the airport saying good-bye, never to see each other again. I might not be hanging out with the same kids all the time in school, but I'm getting to know as much about people of all ages as I am about different countries and foods—and mountains.

As we get ready to go out into the Colorado cold, I'm tempted to tell Tony Tonsing that I already know jumar technique. I learned it at the high-angle rescue course in California—part of my personal prep for Everest. I had called Thor from the airport as I was leaving California, to explain what I had learned. He was surprised and said I was probably the only guy on the Everest trip who knew rescue techniques. Or was an emergency medical technician, for that matter. I was shocked. All these climbers in the most dangerous situations, and so few have any training if something goes wrong. Most people don't even bother. Probably because there are no regulations to force you to have any training at all.

One thing I promised my parents: If they let me go to Everest, I would have the best preparation I could possibly have. Because I was so young, I knew I needed to go into any climbing situation with credentials other climbers would have to recognize and respect. So I took an EMT course at night during the fall and the rescue course on a long weekend in October. The EMT instructor wanted me out because I was only fourteen and I would not even be eligible for my license. (The license allows you to work on an ambulance, makes you eligible for more training for eventual work as a paramedic, but you have to be eighteen.) I got a B, so what could she say? Besides, my purpose was to learn how to apply EMT knowledge to the mountains, not to get a license.

With my training, school, sponsors to call, and homework, I was overwhelmed with work, but it was fascinating to learn about anatomy, medical problems like heart attack and stroke, and typical injuries. And I even learned to stitch wounds—went to a vet and asked if he'd show me. He made me practice on the pigs' feet you can buy in delis. I just wanted to be prepared. What happens, for example, if you're roped up to your partner who's 70 feet above you and he falls, breaks his leg, and is dangling unconscious 500 feet above the ground, held only by your rope for protection?

That's what Mimi taught me in California: how to bring an injured person down so both of you survive. In three days of one-on-one instruction in the desert-hot Buttermilk Mountains, little, strong Mimi showed me how to reach an unconscious climber, clip him into my harness, and rappel down with him as far as I could go, then snake the rope through, establish a new anchor, clip to the rope again, rappel farther, repeating the process until I'm down. You lose a lot of gear and it takes a long time, but you can get down, you can survive!

Mimi was a small dynamo of energy, in her mid-twenties, with dark, short hair. She had such an energetic love for the mountains that she climbed constantly, and turned that experience into teaching, making it fun in the process. One souvenir of Bishop, California, we both shared was the weirdest tan I've ever had. We spent most of the three days hanging in harnesses, with one side of us directly in the 120-degree sun. We wore tank tops, and our left arms and shoulders, exposed to that searing desert sun, were dark reddish brown; our right sides, away from the sun, were almost white!

In addition to rescue techniques, Mimi taught me to jumar as well. In Colorado the ropes are icy, as they will be on Everest. Part of what we learn this long, cold afternoon is to clear the jumar and the rope of ice so the jumar will grip—a long, slow process that involves unclipping from the rope, banging the ice off the rope, and cleaning the teeth of the jumar. Boring work in the icy winds of Ten-Mile Canyon, but all part of the preparation for Everest, which is only two months away.

JANUARY 27, 1995

I'm cramped into a thirteen-hour, knees-to-chin, L.A.-to-Lima, then-to-Buenos Aires flight for my biggest challenge yet: Argentina's Aconcagua. At 23,000 feet, it's the highest mountain in the Western Hemisphere, and a good indicator, says Thor, of my readiness for Everest. But I'm not complaining. As usual, we have to have an airport crisis: Thor was told to check his bag containing all our cameras and expensive equipment. Naturally, the bag did not get on our plane from Denver to L.A. It had to arrive about two minutes before our flight was to depart from the international gate, about a half-mile away. We then had to run, me carrying my ski poles, bag, jacket, and inevitable briefcase full of schoolbooks; Thor stumbling with his heavy equipment bag through L.A. Airport. Thanks to the hour's delay that greeted our sweaty arrival, we made it.

But, as I said, I'm not complaining. Waiting to take the same flight was a group of bubbly, tanned women of all ages, talking and laughing like a group of older Girl Scouts out for a hike. I find out they're the Breast Cancer Survivors' Team, a group of women, all cancer survivors, who will climb Aconcagua to raise money for research. That's why I'm not complaining. Cramped, long flights and lost bags are nothing compared to what these women have gone through. And here they are banding together to climb the same huge mountain I want to summit, and they're raising money in the process. What a great way to celebrate surviving cancer! No wonder they are so happy.

After seeing the Breast Cancer Survivors' Team, I feel bad whining about the roundabout routes of my flights to get to Aconcagua. Think of it: from Boston west to Denver, then farther west and south to L.A., then south and back east to Lima, then south to Buenos Aires, which is more east than New England, and tomorrow back west again to Mendoza, the last city before we get to Aconcagua. Talk about frequent-flier miles!

JANUARY 28, 1995

Buenos Aires is expensive: eight pesos for a glass of orange juice, 144 pesos for an OK hotel room (we needed to find a hotel quickly, especially one that would take our eight barrels of equipment). Not so bad, you might think, because foreign currency is often inflated. Some places you can get a lot of pesos for a dollar. Not here. The peso is worth exactly one American dollar. So the orange juice really cost eight dollars. I didn't spend very much after that, but I could only imagine how fast I could go through all my money here. I bet Snickers bars go for five dollars, Big Macs probably for ten, or a can of soda for six.

As we go through the summer-green countryside on the way back to the airport, Thor gives me a geography quiz. Where is Uruguay? (Across the water from Buenos Aires.) What is Argentina's main export? (Beef.) What country can you see from Aconcagua? (Chile.)

We meet Kip and Norm Smith, a married couple, on the plane to Mendoza. They are on another trip sponsored by Thor's Condor Adventures. Kip and Norm are dressed exactly alike, from shirts to socks and hiking boots. A team, I guess. They've summited the highest points in the United States and now want to branch out. Thor advises Kip about river crossings. "River crossings?" she says. "If my feet get wet, I get instant hypothermia. And what do you have for food? Because I can't eat anything with preservatives." Kip and Norm look like they're going to have a very good time in the Andes.

Lots of good-looking girls in Mendoza, a small city filled with banners announcing soccer tournaments. In the hotel pool, walking along the hot, tree-lined streets, sitting in sidewalk cafés—so many girls I'd love to talk to, if only I had the guts! Thor has work to do before other members of the team get there. So I decide to go early to Puente del Inca, near Aconcagua, with Barry and John, two guys on our team who also came in today to get acclimatized. We start in the thick, humid heat of the oil fields outside Mendoza, then gradually rise into thin, clear mountain air in five hours of dusty bus ride.

Our driver drops us off at Puente del Inca—a beautiful little town at the height of the pass that goes into Chile. There is an ancient house built right over the sulfur hot springs there, where people still go into the water for their health. Puente del Inca also has a military base that must have dark secrets. Outside the gate there's a big sign that says NO PHOTOGRAPHS! For some reason, everybody loves to take pictures of that sign. The Breast Cancer Survivors' Team got to Puente del Inca before us, filling up the only *hosteria* in town. We have no choice but to stay at a hole-in-the-wall little place and listen to the loud Spanish music of Sophia, the woman who tries, without any success, to keep the place clean.

FEBRUARY 1, 1995

John, Barry, and I hiked the local mountain trails the last two days to get acclimated. I suppose I could thank Sophia, the cleaning woman, for our early start. She loves to play the same tape over and over at six A.M. A little revenge: I gave her twelve-year-old son a Metallica tape, which he loves. Now Sophia is listening to heavy metal all day. The rest of our group finally came in; the Breast Cancer Survivors' Team left the *hosteria*; and we had one good night's sleep there before we left this morning for Aconcagua.

Aconcagua presents unusual problems. Although it's the highest mountain in the Western Hemisphere, it's not really a difficult mountain to climb, because it has no glaciers or sheer rock faces. Therefore it attracts a great number of climbers. And that's precisely the problem: many are not experienced enough, fit enough, or acclimated enough to do a 23,000-foot climb. As a result, there are a lot of injuries and deaths from exhaustion, pulmonary and cerebral edemas, dehydration—the big mistakes experienced climbers learn to avoid.

Thor's signing us all in when I make a big mistake of a different sort. Instead of just waiting outside, I have to go into the park office to look around. One of the officers looks up from his desk. "How old are you?" he asks loudly.

The Argentina Park Service is in complete charge of this place, that's for sure. One look at the gate to the state park leading to Aconcagua will tell you that—everything is very well organized. Uniformed park police take your name, passport number, group name, and assign you a number. Then they assign you a plastic garbage bag. You're expected to pick up all your own garbage—and any other garbage you see—before you leave. Until a few years ago, you even had to run a track in your hiking boots to prove you were fit. If you didn't finish the course in a time they liked, no Aconcagua for you.

The officer's voice freezes me as if I've just been caught by border police without a passport. What do I say? Fifteen? Just turned fifteen two weeks ago? Twenty? How about twenty? Thor's busy writing, pretending he doesn't hear this conversation.

"Fifteen," I mumble. I see Thor's head sink as he writes.

"Where are your parents?"

Thor looks up. "His parents are not here. I'm his guardian."

And that starts it. No, Thor doesn't have any papers. Yes, we can get proof. We fax to Mendoza, which is on siesta—an hour's wait—then to Buenos Aires, and on to my parents, who make up a document, notarize it, and get it back to us, giving Thor and me two hours to sit around and wait while the others start the twenty-mile hike to Base Camp. First time since the RI Rock Gym that my age has been a problem. If I hadn't stuck my nose into the office, it wouldn't have been. We finally leave, and Thor laughs at the embarrassed look on my face. "If that's the worst thing that happens, we're in for a good trip," he says, trying to make me feel better.

FEBRUARY 2, 1995

Thor distributes some of the group stuff to save on donkey rentals to Base Camp, and he gives me a five-pound jar of peanut butter. No big deal, except for the fact that I am already carrying an extra twenty-five pounds of schoolbooks nobody knows about! We still have over ten miles to Base Camp. Yesterday we hiked through dusty, rocky trails; today will be more of the same. A hot, dry, long hike. When Thor, Kevin Burn—a doctor in our group—and I stop for lunch, I'm already very warm in just a T-shirt. Two climbers come up to us, dressed in full-length, one-piece down suits—the kind you'd wear at 27,000 feet at 15 degrees below zero. They tell

Thor in Spanish they are from Brazil, flew in yesterday, took a bus up to the park, and, with no acclimatization, went from sea level to 14,000 feet. Why the heavy suits? Beats carrying them, I guess. Geoff Tabin once wore his on the plane coming home from a climb because he had too much baggage.

Kevin insists on checking out these guys, who are just about out of water, sweating and panting for every breath. Kevin takes out his little compact stethoscope and tells one guy he's in bad shape—his heart's racing and he's on the verge of acute mountain sickness. "Look, you continue, you could die! Your body can't get enough oxygen. Get down to a lower altitude. Now!" Sweat dripping from his nose, his eyes glassy, the guy just looks at Kevin. See what I mean? Aconcagua produces a lot of stupid mistakes. Not extreme altitude at this point, but enough to kill this guy because he had not taken the time to acclimatize. His buddy goes off in search of a mule to take them down.

Would I make stupid mistakes? Not likely, you'd think, after all the training I've had. But I do make a stupid mistake. I run out of water. Kevin and Thor are ahead of me. I'm the last of our team, way behind, and I'm hurting. I have a camelback water container—a tube you wear on your back that has a straw you can sip from at any time. The trouble is, you can't tell how much water you have left, particularly on a warm day when you sip a lot. Now I pay. Here I am, the most acclimatized one on the trip, and because I'm weighed down with thirty extra pounds of books and peanut butter, I'm working very hard. Why did I take all these books? To impress the teachers? The algebra book alone must weigh ten pounds. Am I going to do ten pounds' worth of algebra problems? Or read seven pounds of the frilly poems and short stories I'm supposed to "get"? Or study five-and-a-half pounds of history? I even made copies of pages and pages from some books, but I still thought I needed every schoolbook I had. Now that I'm dehydrated to the point where my tongue's sticking to the roof of my mouth, now that I have no more saliva, I wish I had left all the books at home, or at least back in Mendoza.

I go through a flat section of the trail and pass three guys on mules coming down. One's a park guide in uniform; the others are two climbers, zombies staring off into space. The guide tells me in broken English that a third climber had died of exhaustion above Camp Two. Another bad mistake. I should talk. Here I am dehydrated, wasted, and separated from my group because I'm carrying schoolbooks up the highest mountain in the Western Hemisphere.

I sip the last of my water and look off into the distance. I feel the hot wind and see on the brown, dry hills the tiny figures of distant climbers heading for Base Camp, which must be at least another five miles. Am I going to be able to make this? I spot a stream, contaminated by mule droppings, but wet, moist water. I follow it upstream as fast as I can. I have no iodine, no way to purify, but I can wait no longer. I fill the camelback, open the top, and chug about a gallon. I can feel the cool water course through me and sit on a rock to let it digest.

"Hey, punk!" A voice behind me. Has to be George Fuller, a member of our team, the only guy who calls me "punk." "Why stop here? Base Camp's two hundred yards that way."

"What about them?" I nod to the distant climbers on the trail.

"They're heading to Camp One."

George can tell I'm hurting, picks up my pack, says it's twice as heavy as his, and leads me to Base Camp—a little village of tents on the flat brown land, housing maybe two hundred climbers and cooks. We find our tents, and I drink two quarts of Kool-Aid and fall asleep—almost a victim of the same silly mistakes so many seem to make on Aconcagua.

FEBRUARY 8, 1995

So far so good. Three days of rest in Base Camp. Then the rituals of acclimatization: up to Camp Two, back to Base Camp for rest, then up to Camp Two again, and finally here to Camp Three. We take our time. Acclimatize. Minimize mistakes. Climbing Aconcagua's difficult because of the sand. It wears you out. You take a step up and you sink down a step and a half. Snow packs down eventually, but sand just keeps collapsing. Like a nightmare you have when you're a kid. The monster's after you and you can't get away because your feet just keep sinking. That's the feeling I get sometimes climbing Aconcagua. Frustration. So I learn to be patient. Take my time. And now, with better footing up here in the snow of Camp Three—a clean, uncrowded Patio Camp—we're poised to summit.

I'm melting snow for water when I look out the tent door and see a group go by in the driving snow. They are pulling a sled carrying a long bag. "Equipment or dead body?" I ask Kevin.

"Both," he says quietly.

We watch as the three men silently pull the sled off into the gloom of snow.

After dinner, as if to banish thoughts of death, Kevin takes pulses. At 18,000 feet, most guys are in the eighties and nineties. Mine is sixty-four! Such efficiency of the pumping heart! Such superb condition! A wonder in my own time!

"But the question is," says Thor, "is he still alive?" Which gets a big laugh.

Jealous. They're all just jealous.

FEBRUARY 9, 1995

Up at four, in crampons, and up the mountain by a clear dawn whose light casts an unusual orange glow around the shadow of

Aconcagua's summit. As Thor had predicted last night, we make good time across the traverse, which is like walking across the bleachers in the curve of a huge stadium, only the bleachers are for us helpful, firm snow. We are, by now, in full suits, goggles, and heavy mittens in the cold wind. Then to the Canaleta, which Thor said is usually treacherous rock scree (scree is an area of loose rock), more difficult than the sand, but today is made friendly, firm, negotiable, because of snow cover.

Then to the summit. The sheer mass of Aconcagua's summit ridge gives you a chance at a number of false summits—teases that make you think you're there, but you're not. Easy to give in to false summits: if you're tired, cold, why not just say you made it? The real summit can't be much higher than where we are. What difference does it make? Let's head down. Now.

No. Got to find the cross. Then we'll head down. Soon we find the summit. It has a large metal cross with stickers on it and some nut riding around on a mountain bike. Here I am on the highest point in the Western Hemisphere, the highest point I've ever been, looking out to the Andes of Chile and Argentina, huge peaks as far as the eye can see, and some guy's riding around the hard snow whooping and hollering on a mountain bike. He took it apart, carried it up, put it back together, and now is doing some wheelies in the snow. Someone yells that he should ride down the Canaleta. He smiles, says something in Spanish, takes another lap. We get some pictures, congratulate one another, and leave. No great exhilaration this time. As we start down, I feel happy, satisfied, accomplished. But I'm not surprised or overwhelmed. I expected to make it. And I did.

The sun breaks through again, and we're off through the Canaleta and the traverse down to Camp Two, which we reach by two o'clock. Most on our team are tired, want to stop. George, Barry, and I decide to go to Base Camp. We feel strong and want to see if we can do it.

It's dark, and I can barely put one foot in front of the other as I struggle into Base Camp. My feet have been rubbed raw by a layer of dirt that got into my boots and acted like sandpaper. I'm too tired to get my wet clothes off. But I made it. From 18,000 feet to 23,000 feet, down to 14,000 feet in one day—from five A.M. to six P.M., my personal-best preparation for Everest. That's all any of this is: preparation for Everest. Maybe it's like when a baseball team wins the playoffs, gets into the World Series, and you see the players interviewed. They're quietly glad for what they've done but won't really celebrate till they win the big one. Am I excited about 23,000 feet? Not really. It was an easy climb, complicated only by problems of attention and endurance. Aconcagua proves I'm ready for the next step—Everest. I've got the endurance, strength, and ability, I tell myself as I finally strip off my wet clothes and dry off and fall asleep.

FEBRUARY 10, 1995

We hike out, the longest twenty miles I've ever hiked. It seems easy, though, even with the schoolbooks, because I'm in such a relaxed, tired glow. We get to Puente del Inca around seven, and when we find a driver of a small bus willing to take us to Mendoza, we crowd everything in for a five-hour ride to long showers and comfortable beds. Then I sit up at 2:38 A.M. in Mendoza, Argentina, and smile when I realize that when I get home, my schoolmates will be just beginning a week off for winter break. Timing is everything, isn't it?

the north side

I'm standing in the courtyard of the Summit Hotel, duct tape in one hand, a ripped tent in the other. The afternoon sun blazes down, and the haze and din of Kathmandu traffic drifts in from the street like fog. As I look around me at the blue plastic barrels littering the ground, I wonder how far away Everest still is.

Thor, Javier, and I are repairing equipment for the expedition. Must be twenty-five barrels out here. Some contain meat Thor bought and froze in Denver, now packed in Styrofoam chips and still frozen two weeks later. Others contain tents, personal equipment, clothes, rope: everything spread out for inspection and repair. Boring for them, but fun for me, to be working with these guys as they tell climbing stories and talk about the mountains. Fun for me, too, is our first night in Kathmandu, showing Javier around, bringing him to my favorite restaurant. Usually it's Javier who leads me into new travels, but the other night, jet lag and all, I was the sophisticated veteran of Kathmandu. An afternoon shower comes through, and we race around to get everything under cover. Then the sun comes out, the skies wiped clean by the rain, and suddenly we can see the distant mountains around us everywhere, far off but huge and snow-capped, as if during the rain someone had moved new backdrops into our movie set, giving us renewed motivation to get out there. We duct-tape ripped tents and check out ropes, scattering our equipment over every inch of the courtyard as we prepare for our summit bid on the north side of Mount Everest.

Mount Everest creates the border between Nepal, on the south side, and Tibet, on the north side. The very first attempt to climb Everest, by the legendary George Mallory and Andrew Irvine in 1924, was made from the north. (No one knows if they made it: they died on the mountain.)

Why try to climb the north side today? It's less expensive, for one thing. A tightly budgeted expedition like ours, with the same format, food, and time frame, costs about $18,000 per person on the northern, or Tibet, side, and about $24,000 on the southern, or Nepal, side. Our expedition is not for those who may need help in getting up the mountain. In fact, we'll be expected to work right along with the Sherpas. Even the expense for porters and yaks is far less—you can drive right up to Base Camp and need yaks for only three days to Advanced Base Camp. On the south side, you face two weeks of hiking, with porters and yaks, just to get to Base Camp.

And of course the north side is far more challenging—or, as some might say, dangerous. I read a lot about Everest, particularly the north route. I talked to a lot of climbers and watched videos. Here are some of the "challenges" we'll be facing: Because it is in the shadow of the mountain much of the day, with the winds over the north ridge swooping down constantly, the north side of Everest is much colder. The route generally is steeper than the south side, and the chances for frostbite, pulmonary or cerebral edema, and altitude exhaustion are far greater because of the very remoteness of the terrain. Base Camp is at 17,000 feet; Advanced Base Camp at 21,000 feet. However, to get from one to the other is a grueling 18-mile hike. If you have an accident at ABC or above, you have a very big problem; there's just no way to get off the mountain. Helicopters can't come to the rescue, as they can on the south side. The nearest hospital is probably 500 miles away. Even if everything goes well, you can't rest properly at 21,000 feet, so you have to get down to Base Camp more than a few times—a trip that may not be dangerous, but, at 18 high-altitude miles each way, is exhausting.

So far, only sixty-seven climbers have summited from the north side; maybe seven hundred have tried it. I don't think that necessarily makes the north side of Everest dangerous—as if it is a monster ready to reach out and grab you in its jaws. But the north side of Everest *is* a challenge, and, as I stand here in the heat of the Summit courtyard, I know I'm ready.

Before I left, people at home would ask me why I was going, and, as simple as it sounded, I had to say: because I want to climb Everest. Not to become the youngest necessarily; just to climb it. I learned that I needed an edge with sponsors, a marketing point to attract their financial support, so I emphasized going for the record of being the youngest. But my main goal will always be the climbing. Not the record, not the publicity. Summiting. I'd rather climb in obscurity.

Since September, I have had anything but obscurity. First, I was interviewed by Paula Zahn on *CBS This Morning*. She smiled at me and asked me questions about being the youngest to climb Everest. So what did I do? Sat staring straight at the camera, mumbling in a monotone. I still can't remember a thing I said. Some national TV debut. People probably thought I was still frozen from being up in the mountains too long.

That same day, an article came out in the *Providence Journal* about my Everest trip. The reporter, Chris Rowland, had interviewed me and my parents, written about my training, my parents' support, the opportunity to go. But he soured the whole thing by quoting Rick Wilcox, a well-known New Hampshire climber, who had summited Everest. Rick said that I was far too young, that my going to Everest was a form of child abuse. He had somehow formed the opinion that my parents were forcing me to go to Everest. All my parents' friends, all the people at school who'd encouraged my trips, now had a thought in their heads from Rhode Island's only major paper that my parents were child abusers. How could I deal with that? Or my parents? Deny child abuse? They had no answer for such an absurd accusation.

Then another article came out, even more upsetting, this one an AP story that went out to many papers about my bid for Everest. This writer had a quote from Sir Edmund Hillary, the man who first summited Everest in 1953, who has devoted his life to the mountain as guardian, historian, and expert. "A fifteen-year-old boy has no right to be on the summit, because these large expeditions are merely conveying people up the mountain." Those words shocked me, considering that back in '53 he had about two hundred porters for his team! Don't get me wrong. Hillary deserves a lot of credit as the first, but he has a lot of responsibility, too—his words are considered golden. He doesn't even know me! Or my abilities. In the same article, Glenn Porzak, president of the American Alpine Club, said he wouldn't bring an eighteen-year-old to Everest, never mind a fifteen-year-old. Fifteen was too young; could never carry his own weight.

The top people in the climbing world were calling my parents child abusers and saying I couldn't pull my own weight on Everest. At first I was furious; I had worked so hard, and I was being written about like some phony who doesn't belong on the mountain. Then I went for a long run, came home, and thought, Who cares? Hillary is very possessive of the mountain, and probably feels that any new record—as mine would be—takes away from him. Porzak has no idea of who I am or what I'm like. And child abuse? This whole Everest thing is my idea, not theirs! My parents and I talked about inviting Hillary, Porzak, and Wilcox for dinner after I summited. The menu? Crow.

Finally, a reporter called Al Burgess, my climbing mentor. Al told me he lit into him. "You ever have a dream? Probably not," he said. "Probably never thought it possible. Here's a kid going out to do his dream and all you guys can do is write something bad about him." After that, I read even more positive comments from Al and from Thor. Both of them defended me in print, saying I was ready.

Then there seemed to be even more positives. ESPN called my last day at school, wanting to film me in class. OK, I said, and by that afternoon there were four camera crews following me around school—ESPN and three local stations. My classmates were goofing around, and great-looking senior girls, teachers, people I didn't know, all suddenly became my friends. Jocks, cheerleaders, everybody—wishing me luck and smiling into the camera. Girls hung out of windows, yelling, "We love you, Mark!" and everyone asking, "Are you scared?" "Is it dangerous?" I didn't like the cameras in my face, but I must admit that at least it was positive.

So was *NBC Nightly News*, which sent Roger O'Neil to do a segment on me before we left Denver. He had Thor and me all over the place, climbing, running, and, of course, talking—all which I did so much easier than on CBS earlier.

Porzak and others had said young people have a hard time at altitude. I read a book on high-altitude physiology by Dr. Peter Hackett and called him in Alaska to get his opinion. He said I was as able as any twenty-five-year-old of comparable size. "If young kids don't do well at altitude," he said, "it's because they don't know how to pace themselves, to acclimatize."

The topic of child abuse was still in my mind. My grandfather is the oldest living graduate of the FBI Academy and still has contacts, so my mom always had him check out all my expedition leaders. My mother often went with me during training: to New York for ice climbing, to California for high-angle rescue, to visit me in Denver just before we left to come here. My father and I discussed every bit of training, equipment, and sponsors.

My mother was quoted in one article asking these questions: "Why would we stop him? How could we stop him? If he has such burning desires, should we stop his dreams?" Her answer was always no to those questions, and, instead of stopping me, she and my father insisted that I stick to my training schedule no matter what. On those cold, rainy nights when I wanted to stay home, my father would grab the keys to the car to drive me to the hospital to do stairs. "The mountain is very unforgiving," he'd say. "You want to take on Everest, you have to be ready. Otherwise don't go." That's not child abuse. Nor is it child abuse when parents swallow their own fear and nervousness to give their kid the opportunity to take on the greatest mountain in the world. All parents have to let go of their kids, support them in things they'd never dare try themselves.

"We have to get all this stuff out of here by tonight." Thor breaks through my thoughts. His face is streaked with sweat and dirt, and he's slumped over with the thought of organizing such a mess. "Some big Nepali official is coming for an event and we have to be out of here." So that's what we do: clean it up as fast as we can. Preparation. Work that never shows up anywhere. That's what more than half of an Everest expedition seems to be. I've been gone from home for over three weeks, and I'm only as far as Kathmandu. Some of the roads to Tibet are blocked by avalanches; our team is still not here; we're patching tents in a courtyard; and I haven't worked out or had exercise in a very long time. Even my meeting with Geoff Tabin got screwed up. Geoff is over here working for the World Health Organization, doing eye surgery in the mountains. I hadn't seen him since our RI Rock Gym climbing days. We'd stay in touch by phone, but it was going to be great to see him—especially here, just before my Everest bid. I wanted to show him how far I'd come in two years and to thank him for getting me started on the way.

But no. He went to the Mustang Holiday Inn hours before we were supposed to meet. All I got was a note saying he waited, but had to go. A mix-up somewhere.

Waiting and patience: that's the theme so far. I had gone to Denver early to train and to acclimatize, then spent a lot of time there waiting around for Thor and Javier to do errands. That's what happens when you're fifteen and can't drive. You wait.

Maybe learning patience is a good thing. Slows you down a bit. If those TV cameras and my high school "friends" could see me lugging the barrels around in the afternoon sun, they'd see a different side of what goes into climbing Everest.

MARCH 30, 1995

At last we're on the way! Who cares if yesterday we were jammed into a bus to take us to the Tibetan border. Or that Kodari, the last town in Nepal, was only a few dust-covered buildings. Or that once we crossed the Freedom Bridge into Tibet we had to wait to find transportation to Zhangmu. That's the way it is at the Tibet border: just grab the first truck. Kind of like hitchhiking. One guy stands out on the road, and everyone else hides behind a wall until someone stops. Then nine climbers and seven Sherpas carrying thirty barrels jump on, too. (A little exaggeration maybe, but not much.)

We found an open truck willing to take us, piled in the back, and soon we were bouncing up into the mountains, watching the monkeys in the trees, plunging up and down sharp switchbacks—really moving. Everest wouldn't be long now, right? Wrong. Up in the mountains at Zhangmu, the real checkpoint, the border guards checked every piece of equipment—every oxygen bottle—all day and all night while we stayed in Zhangmu's falling-down hotel. More patience.

This morning we load our stuff into Toyota 4Runners provided by the Chinese government as part of our license fee, and we manage to get a few miles down the road before we're stopped by a forest fire, a huge wall of flame. It's in the distance, but I guess close enough to force the road to be closed for about three hours. Everest will melt before I get to it!

We bounce up into the mountains and finally begin to feel we're getting someplace. That someplace is miles of barren hills of dirt, so dusty you have to keep a handkerchief over your face to breathe, so dusty that when you get out of the truck for a break, you wear dust in every nook and cranny of your clothes. Next, that someplace is a mile-long path cut through a snowfield just wide enough for a truck, with snowbanks towering eight or ten feet higher scraping the rearview mirrors. Other times that someplace is a seven-foot-wide muddy road, snaking along a cliff—with a 1,000-foot wall on one side and a 2,000-foot drop-off on the other. Sometimes you wait for a Tibetan crew to break up and clear fallen rocks, or you may have to help porters transfer everything across a washout—careful to avoid slipping off the edge of the slimy, wet road—then reload it onto new trucks. Then you ride about a mile to the next rock slide and carry everything across another treacherous area, into yet another set of trucks.

All you can see are dirt and rocks, as far as the eye can see. Dirt and rocks—rounded mountains of them, or long straightaways. And in the distance, so far away it seems like a white mirage that gets no closer, is our goal: Everest. Distance is numbing out here. (As is sitting in the back seat of a small truck. I ask Tony Tonsing, sitting in the luxury of stretched-out legs in the front seat, to change places for a while. "No" is his sharp response. Sign of troubles to come? Hope not.)

Often fifty, sixty miles pass between any signs of life, human or otherwise. The humans you do see, Tibetans, are far different from the Nepali. Nepali smile, welcome you to their teahouses or their homes. The Tibetans stare at you as you pass by them on the road, as if they are suspicious of any strangers. Because many of them are nomadic, setting up camps in canvas tents—as much on the move as you are—you hardly ever see them, much less talk with them, except to trade stuff like bottles for yak bells.

APRIL 8, 1995

Nyalam, like so many other places we go through, is not much to look at. Almost like a small town you'd see in a Clint Eastwood western. The good guy, Clint Eastwood, comes riding slowly into the sad, small town, in the middle of nowhere, the wind whirling dust around him. A small dog yelps at his horse's feet; the wind bangs the loose shutter of the hotel; the heroine peers from a grimy window; the bad guys sit in the saloon waiting to make a move. That's what Nyalam seems like to me.

Which brings up a delicate point. Stench. Reeking, obnoxious, outhouse stink. All those westerns don't give us a clue, but if Nyalam is like a town in the old West, I'm glad I didn't live there. All Nyalam has for a toilet facility is a little wooden building with a wooden platform and a hole. You have to get used to it if you want to travel. It's just going to stink. Something awful. When I was a little kid I remember cleaning manure out of a barn, putting on big boots, taking a pitchfork to the huge, squishy pile, with the ammonia smell so strong it would make me sick. That's what it's like in just about every place we go. Compound that by traveling in a large group, so that everyone is not only competing for the privilege of using the place but very much aware of the previous occupant's presence. It makes you wish you could wait till you got home—at the end of May.

The team really has not had a chance to come together yet. We've been split into three groups, riding all day in trucks. At night, we're still very quiet with one another, friendly enough, but not really together yet. I don't think Roger Gocking has accepted me. I know he's a very experienced climber who hates whiners who don't do their share. There has been no big test of anyone yet, including me. But Ray Dorr has already had words with Tonsing. Ray Dorr is a thick, short guy with a pale face, red hair, and a red beard. He works on Broadway, building sets for shows like *Phantom of the Opera* and *Les Misérables*. And he has a temper. In Kathmandu, we were walking out of the hotel and Tony, whom we've already named Socrates because he knows so much about everything, was rattling on about something the way he does. Ray turned around to him, pointed his finger in Tony's face, and said, "You! Shut up!" If something like that happened with kids my age, you'd have a big fight. But Tony did. Shut up.

APRIL 11, 1995

I can see Everest!

I'm standing on the roof of the hotel in Shegar, our last stop before Base Camp, having climbed the fire-escape ladder to get up here. From here I look out over the hills, then to the ridges rising more sharply, then to the snow-covered peaks, and finally to Everest itself, its north face a terrible beauty of black rock speckled with white, its plume of wind-driven snow trailing gracefully off to the south as it rises above a whole landscape of other mountains clustered, it seems, in its protective mass. While Everest dominates my vision, I realize that my position on the roof of the hotel gives me an unusual perspective. Unusual because it symbolizes so much of Tibet. On one side I look up at an ancient monastery-fortress, or *dzong*, which is a series of buildings built into the spine of a mountain like a series of steps, where monks for hundreds of years spent their lives in prayer, far removed from the town. Around me are the plain, flat stucco houses of the town, and beyond them are the tinroofed administration buildings of the occupying Chinese authorities. And nowhere a sign of trees or vegetation, only the barren, brown hills. Tibet's past, present, and future in one quick view.

APRIL 13, 1995

Base Camp. Russell Brice, the New Zealand climber, owns his own expedition company and has led climbers here so often that he rules the roost in Base Camp. He greets our dusty caravan and directs us to set up camp about a quarter of a mile away from the few teams already here. Base Camp. Sounds so permanent, so solid. A place. A destination where you get all your gear out of the trucks, shake off the dust, and move in. Actually, it's just more of the same rocks and dirt with one more element: glacier ice. We build our tent bases on white rocks that are on top of melting, changing, shifting glacier ice. Not that we have much choice.

I clear and level a spot for my tent. As I clear away small rocks, dig into the dirt with my hands to smooth the foundation for my tent base, I accidentally scoop up an old syringe. The needle point is dull; it's been there, no doubt, for years. But a rude welcome to Everest Base Camp for me. After thousands of miles and many days of travel into one of the world's most remote regions, I almost stab myself with a dirty needle. I look around and see evidence of other souvenirs of climbers' presence: white toilet paper, unfurled in the wind. White man's prayer flags, the Sherpas call it, because it does not biodegrade out here. Assorted plastic containers, plus other stuff left over from last year's expeditions. Sad to say, but in one of the world's most remote areas, there is more of a problem with garbage than in some big cities. Most climbers are certainly sensitive to the environment, but there are no rules about "carry in, carry out" as there were in NOLS, so at the conclusion of an Everest expedition the place is a mess.

Not many in Base Camp to mess things up yet. Paul Phau's American team came in early to set ropes, acclimatize, and organize their vast amount of equipment for a successful summit bid. This team got here early enough to catch one of the last winter storms, so strong it blew a tent away. At the time, some guy was all soaped up in the shower (showers are primitive; just heated water in a bucket), and wham! the whole tent was gone, leaving him with only the soap to keep him warm.

How Reinhardt Patscheider joined our expedition is a good example of how climbers sometimes get together on these ventures. Most climbers are on teams formed in their own countries, some commercial (meaning we pay to have Thor lead us); others are sponsored by a country or organization. And some climbers are like Reinhardt. Two of Thor's friends own a German international mountain company and bought half of the license Thor owned. These friends sold off most of the available spots on the trip to a group of Latvians, who will be here soon. Reinhardt was able to get one of the remaining positions and will climb solo. He's an experienced 8,000-meter peak climber from North Tirol, who survived a horrible fall going for the summit on Annapurna. I read that he fell over 800 feet down an ice face and managed to brake himself just before he went over a cliff.

APRIL 15, 1995

We talk, play backgammon, read, do little but breathe. It's important to lie around at first while the body adjusts to altitude; after all, just walking to the dining tent is work, leaving you huffing as if you were running. Four of us got more exercise than we bargained for this afternoon when we decided to hike down to Rongbuk Monastery, only two miles (we figured) below us. Greg Miller, the lawyer; Dr. Jim Wheeler; Reinhardt Patscheider; and I wanted to see how the monks live at 17,000 feet, in the world's highest religious establishment. The hike to the monastery was far longer than we had thought, almost eight miles each way and far beyond what we were prepared for. But it was worth it.

Once in the monastery, it was easy for me to see how these monks keep so spiritual. In the large, open courtyard, I could hear the monks chanting. I looked around at the plain painted walls and up at the clean, deep sky, heard the rush of wind from the mountains, and realized that's all there is here. No vegetation, not even a store to buy anything for a hundred miles. Nothing to stand between you and what the Buddhists call enlightenment. When the chanting ended, the monks came out to the courtyard to stare at us. Their plain robes and clear eyes told me how content they were in the simplicity of their lives. Then they began to talk to each other, pointing at us and giggling, happy to have visitors.

One young monk, not much older than I, looked at me and whispered in the ear of an old man standing next to him. He pointed at me, nodded, and smiled. I nodded back, wanted to talk to him, ask him what it's like living caged up here your whole life, wearing the same old pants and robe, eating the same food, praying day in and day out, so close to Everest and never able to get closer to its summit. Or anywhere else, for that matter. Then I wondered who really had the best deal: a kid like me, standing there in my fancy hiking clothes, traveling thousands of miles, ready to take on Everest, or that guy, probably ready to spend all the years ahead right here at the foot of Everest, praying.

I wasn't sure, am still not sure. We're both young, strong, and committed to what we do. Maybe I can learn as much climbing as he does praying. Maybe he's as happy praying as I am in the mountains. Maybe we both have a good deal. The bell was rung (an old, empty climber's oxygen tank), and he turned to go. We bowed toward each other and waved, almost as if we had talked. Whenever I think of getting closer to God on my pilgrimages to the mountains, I'll always think of this place, already closer to heaven than any other house of prayer could be, and the look on the face of that young monk.

APRIL 18, 1995

My first steps on Everest were like throwing out the first ball on opening day, or the first scene of a world-premiere movie, or the first day of school. Because it's the highest mountain in the world, it should be somehow different, pink maybe, or big neon signs everywhere—something. But starting up the long trail from Base Camp to our first intermediate camp, I feel Everest rising not so much to a sharply angled summit before me but more like a massive ocean wave of rock and snow.

How do I feel on opening day? Confident. You never want to think that this mountain is going to beat you. You think in terms of steps, segments, little sections of a big plan, which will add up to making the summit. We climb this clear, cool morning to the first of two intermediate camps. These are just for acclimatizing, for storing a few things. They're places to measure our progress. Remember, Advanced Base Camp, where we'll spend most of our time, is 18 miles away and 4,000 vertical feet above Base Camp. If our goal is to get comfortable enough to stay at 21,000 feet, we have to be very careful to do it right.

Here's the plan: The first ascent to ABC (Advanced Base Camp) will take three days because of stops at each of the intermediate camps. Each of those days will be rest days, especially at ABC, where we'll spend an extra day before coming back down. The next trip up, sometime next week, we'll take only two days to get to ABC. Then eventually we'll be able to do the 18 miles to ABC in one very long day. Once set up at ABC (the Sherpas stay the whole two months here), we'll come down to Base Camp for occasional rests, but most of the rest of our time will be at 21,000 feet. But ABC is only the beginning of the story, because it is really our Base Camp—just a very high one. Camp One is actually 2,000 steep feet above ABC at the North Col; Camp Two is another 3,000 feet up the North Ridge; and the last, Camp Three, is just below the Northeast Ridge, about 2,000 feet higher than Camp Two.

Two months of one step at a time, two months of strategically planned moves, will get me and our whole team to the summit. Seems funny to think of all the wind, cold, angles of rock and ice, the possibility of injury and sickness, and to reduce it all to a cold, calculated game plan. But that's what I'm thinking on opening day as Kat, Thor, and I start up toward the first intermediate camp.

What I don't want to think about, what I block from my mind, is our team, how it gets along, what will happen. Thor has to wait for his girlfriend, Kat, to get ready. Because we three are the last to leave, we get to carry forgotten items like extra rope. Fifteen minutes after we start, Kat complains that her pack is too heavy for her.

Even though I'm loaded with my own pack and extra equipment, I offer to help. For some reason, what she gives me to carry really bothers me: what seems like ten pounds of cosmetic facial creams. I take it, say nothing, but can't help but wonder what the rest of the expedition will be like if we have to wait for Kat, who insists on taking ten pounds of facial creams up Mount Everest and then can't carry them herself.

As we hike along, I'm thinking about the dinner we had in Denver. My mother had come out to see us off and had taken everyone out to dinner: Javier; his wife, Charro; Thor; his parents; and me. Missing? Kat. She had to have her nails done.

APRIL 21, 1995

Advanced Base Camp. Late-night headache. Throbbing, hurt-your-eyes, don't-move-too-fast headache. Difficult to move at all up here at 21,000 feet, never mind with any speed. Never stayed overnight this high before. But that's not why my head hurts. Hate to admit it, but I have no pillow. My head lolls around on my piled-up clothes and I can't sleep. And yak bells going off like gongs every two seconds.

Just like my first trip to Nepal. Perfectly still night. Yaks asleep. And their bells just keep on clanging.

ABC is on a jumble of rocks on a glacier, which gives an already cold night that extra jolt of air-conditioning you just don't need. We helped the Sherpas set up the cook tent and dining tent, then carved out flat places for our own tents and went to bed early. What I call Sherpa cockroach pace—go fast for twenty minutes, rest for five—got me up here pretty fast from intermediate camp. I am tired now but still can't sleep.

Greg Miller is a talkative, energetic guy who joined our team late, but he had so many climbing stories I never doubted that he was experienced. Not till we started to climb. After a couple of hours climbing on snow and ice, a climber not familiar with crampons will tire and his feet will start to turn in, the points of the crampons catching the material on the other leg. Pretty soon the insides of the pants' legs are shredded. Maybe that's what happened to Greg coming up the steep snow sections today.

But that's not why I can't sleep. I'm sharing a tent with Greg, and he spilled water all over my stuff. Water, I should tell you, is hard to come by up here. If you carry it up, it freezes solid. You have to melt snow. You set up a gas stove and feed snow into the pot until you get enough. But snow doesn't produce much water. A gallon can take you three hours to melt. And a gallon doesn't go very far, because you have to drink tons to avoid dehydration.

Worse than wasting the water is spilling it all over my stuff, getting it soaked, turning it to slush. Apologies don't make up for carelessness up here. Neither does, an hour later, spilling your pee bottle all over the same stuff I just dried out! Pee bottles are a necessary fact of tent life. Kind of like when you're in the hospital and not allowed to get up. It's so much better to go into a bottle inside your warm sleeping bag than to go outside and risk frostbite on any number of extremities—as long as you put the pee-bottle cover on tight, which Greg did not. But these mistakes are not the problem; they could happen to anyone. I'm awake wondering about a lot of other things.

I thought coming here that this would be like most of my other trips, with everyone committed to the same thing—especially on Everest. But I'm seeing little cracks in the structure. Thor spends a lot of time with Kat, who seems to always stare into space, sulking as if she doesn't want to be here. Carlo Rocca, a triple-bypass survivor, is mad as hell that the private Sherpa Thor promised him is at home, sick. Pat Caffrey is already having respiratory problems.

Even Reinhardt got sick and left Base Camp to go back to Kathmandu, with a promise to return. Roger Gocking doesn't like me, I can tell. The Latvians, about eight of them, joined us at Base Camp, then felt comfortable enough to eat our food (dumping our A.1. steak sauce on every potato they could find). At Base Camp, too, Tibetan yak herders come into the kitchen tent and steal anything they can before our Sherpas scare them off. I know I'm whining, I know I'm a little homesick, but cracks in the structure, no matter how small, have a way of growing, and that's what bothers me.

Despite all the problems, nothing can take away from being on this mountain. I don't know if those monks in Rongbuk Monastery ever get used to the blood-red sunsets and the ten shades of gray in the afternoon clouds, but I sure don't. I wonder if the Sherpas ever take for granted avalanches like the one I saw this afternoon. I heard it first, like a big truck growling down the mountain in low gear, and then I saw it—a white crest splashing like a waterfall down a distant slope. And tonight, around nine, I stood outside my tent and looked around. Above me was the night-black sky punched with brilliant pinholes of white stars. Below, far below, near where I knew Rappi La to be (the pass between Everest and the small mountains that lead to Nepal), I could see the flash and glimmer of silent lightning storms. Selfish as it sounds, I was glad to be alone when I saw it. Same with the avalanche. Same with Everest itself. You may be with a team, but you climb alone, summit alone, experience it alone.

Base Camp is filling up. Thor says soon there'll be almost two hundred climbers and their support people, a total of almost four hundred, before the season's over. ABC has four more teams due up tomorrow. All those people wanting the same thing I do. How many climbers can fit on the summit of Everest? That's like asking how many angels can you fit on the head of a pin. I used to imagine all these angels falling off the sides of the pin. Same image of Everest. Two hundred climbers all at the top at the same time, guys falling off the edge. But that's not the way it is. It's all mine. No matter what cracks in the structure, or who likes me or not, it's up to me to keep pushing myself to the summit, to focus on every careful step. No blaming anyone else. No excuses. It's up to me.

everest '95

CHAPTER TEN

APRIL 23, 1995

If ever you wanted to make a movie of climbing Everest, here would be a spectacular opening scene. Start with a panoramic view of the cold, black, familiar Everest peak, its graceful plume trailing away into the jet stream. Pan slowly down so the camera finds the North Ridge of Everest, showing on one side the sheer black rock face, marbled by snow, and the tranquil world of glittering, slanted white, angled below a deep blue sky, with a full flash of sun. Let the camera find a small group of tiny tents huddled just below the edge of the snow line on the ridge. Zoom the lens into focus on a tiny string of black dots slowly moving up the slant of white snow toward the tents. Move in slowly enough to give viewers the sense of enormous expanse the dots are trying to travel through. Zoom in closer and closer so the viewers can see the dots transformed into humans in bright colors. Listen for the gasps for breath, the crunch of snow, the otherwise deep quiet. Let the viewer try to take in the scale of size of mountain to puny little humans crawling up its sharp angle.

By the way, that'd be me down there. Third from the end. First group.

WOW! Twenty-three thousand feet up! In teams of six, on fixed ropes, in bright, late-morning windless sunshine, crunching on firm Styrofoam snow with crampons on steep grade, with a view that bumps up mountain peaks in wave after choppy wave into the distance. We make our way to Camp One. Roger, Pat, Greg, Javier, Ray, and I are ahead of Thor, Tony, Carlo, Kat, Jim, and Mike Roth. We keep a steady but slow pace; I feel good, but I'm getting very tired. And I thought I was acclimatized!

So what, tired. We're almost to Camp One, and when we stop to rest, I can look down into what seems the very soul of Tibet, the glaciers like wide, smooth highways, the brown valleys and mounds of hills so far below. If I stop to think how high I am, I won't be able to take another step. But, of course, I do—take another step, and another, and another, linked as I am by fixed rope to the other members of the team.

I wish the team members were always linked so well. I saw more signs of cracks in the structure when we were building our dining table and chairs yesterday in Advanced Base Camp. Ray, who has a hand injury, struggled with the heavy rocks. But he still worked hard until Tony, who put himself in charge, rejected Ray's work. So Ray spouted off, fuming about working with jerks like Tony. Reminded me of the quilts. We all bought similar quilts in Kathmandu for our tents. Got to Base Camp and everybody started arguing over them. As if the quilts were all different. Just like little kids. And then Kat didn't want to climb, so, of course, Thor had to wait until the mood struck her so they could get up to ABC. I hope the mood strikes her often.

More important to focus on the dazzling day before me. I should just be glad I'm up here with Thor, because he encouraged me to do all the climbing in South America, encouraged me to be here now. I've learned more from him than any one person, and if he wasn't there to teach me, Javier was.

Camp One is a great place to learn the contrasts of black and white on Everest firsthand. Come out of your tent and you look down the white, steep, snow-covered rock face to the familiar glacier and valley below. As wild and as difficult as it seems to climb, you know it's possible—after all, you just did it. Down there, other people are preparing to do the same thing. Now climb 10 feet up the snowpack and look over the edge of the North Ridge: you get a very different feeling. The blast of icy wind tears at your face as you stare down the bald, black rock face that seems to go for miles almost straight down. It's like looking into death. And then you realize, while the wind is throwing you around, that you better get used to looking at the black and the white, because as you go higher up the mountain and climb along the two-foot-wide knife-edge of the ridge, one mistake can throw you down the bottomless black rock or send you sliding down the white slope of snow and ice. In either case, a mistake could be fatal. It's right there in black and white.

APRIL 26, 1995

Base Camp. Sleeping late because I came down from Advanced Base Camp yesterday—all 18 miles—in one long day. Stiff, sore, legs dead. But I made it. I come out of my tent to see Javier, Mike Roth, and Jim Wheeler all packing up to leave. Not for Advanced Base Camp, but for home. Javier says he's sick; Roth complains about the food; Wheeler just wants out. Not unusual to see guys quit climbing. The failure rate is always high on Everest. For whole expeditions, the failure rate over the years is above 60 percent, so imagine what it is for individuals. Kind of like the NBA. How many high school basketball players ever play college? How many of them make it to the pros? Same on Everest. The experienced Everest climbers tell me many quit for any number of reasons: illness, fatigue, intimidation, the loss of will. They also tell me you can't start questioning yourself, that you can't think, If that guy can't make it, what chance do I have?

It is unusual, however, for people just to get up and leave altogether. Most stay around, cheer on their teammates, help in Base Camp. These guys just get into a Jeep and leave. Roth, a charter jet pilot in his other life, says he's got only $400 to his name. Says he's going to join a monastery. About right for a guy who leaves because there's no lemonade. (We do have a bit of a food problem, actually. At other camps, you eat all you want—just to sustain energy up in altitude. Our tent always has a familiar cry of "Don't eat all that at once.") Jim Wheeler just wanted out. Did about all he could do. Feels satisfied. I'm not sure if Javier is sick or intimidated. Javier has been to 23,000 feet many times in South America. But when he did, he always looked down from a summit. Maybe he can't cope with the idea of looking up at 6,000 feet more to climb. But who isn't intimidated? You have to keep your mind focused on the small, individual steps.

As we say good-bye and good luck, I almost wish I were going with them. I've been away for years, it seems. I miss my bed, my mom's meals, my father, my dogs. As the Jeep crawls away in the dust, my list keeps getting longer and longer. TV, music, showers, clean clothes, green grass, trees. I can't help it. Home. Those guys are heading back to all that, and I feel the way that young monk I met at Rongbuk Monastery must feel when visitors leave—am I doing the right thing staying here?

Later that day my question is answered by a simple visit to Paul Phau's American Base Camp. There I meet Emily, the friendly, talkative lady who helps run the camp. We sit at the table in her warm dining tent, eating chocolate-chip cookies, and soon I'm talking about my mom and dad and we're laughing about my new puppy. George Mallory's grandson from Australia is on this particular expedition, which was planned to commemorate his grandfather's climb seventy years ago. I ask Emily if I should tell the younger Mallory that my parents commemorated his grandfather, too—by naming a dog after him. This camp, like Emily herself, takes the boredom right out of Base Camp. The members of the team invite me to dinner, and we laugh and joke so much that I forget about that Jeep to the freedom I really don't want. Besides, they give me a whole can of Pringles potato crisps and a roll of soft, soft toilet paper!

APRIL 30, 1995

Everest stands between any little ray of warmth from the sun and us. We're at 25,000 feet, on our way to Camp Two, crampons digging into the hard snow of the steep, windblown North Face. The wind is howling, so strong that I wear a full down suit, carrying a downhill ski pole in one hand and an uphill ice ax in the other for balance as I angle up the steep face, tacking like a sailboat into the crosswind.

If I take my time and block out the sound, and don't let my mind think of images of leaves being plucked off trees by cold autumn winds, I will be fine. If I keep my balance and maintain a solid pace, keeping the same distances between Tony and Greg above me and Thor and Kat below me, I'll be fine. If only my hands were warmer, if only my thumbs weren't numbing up. I know the problem: thumbs in the straps of pole and ax gradually have their circulation cut off, even in warmer weather. Today they are exposed to frostbite. I have a decision to make.

"I'm going down!" I yell to Thor, and point to my thumb. What the hell. Always easier to give in to something that's really bothering you, something that could be dangerous. Why push through it? Why risk losing thumbs? Just to keep going? Just to look good? No. I don't want to jeopardize anything. He nods; he understands.

"I'll go with you," Greg shouts against the wind. "I've had enough for today."

"Don't do that," I shout back. I don't need his help—don't want anyone to go down just because I am, or not summiting because I'm not. "Don't use me for an excuse to be easy on yourself!" I shout back at Greg.

"I know. But it's the first trip up and I don't have any energy, so . . ."

I shake my head in disgust at Greg's excuses and head down to Advanced Base Camp to get my thumbs warm. All the way down, Greg trailing behind me, I keep asking myself: Am I being too easy on myself, as I think Greg is? I know my instincts are right. I know I'll always deal with a dangerous situation with my head. But I have to know I won't be so easy on myself. I didn't run stairs late at night, or run ten-milers, or do 1,000-rep workouts to come over here and be easy on myself. Never!

I'm way ahead of Greg, going so fast with the wind at my back I can feel the blood pulse through my thumbs well before I get to Advanced Base Camp. My thumbs will be fine, but I'm still mad about what happened. At first I'm not sure why. Why should I care if Greg turns back? I stop to rest, to look back up to the summit. Then it hits me. If I want to get there, what I always have to do, no matter what, is be absolutely sure I know the difference between being easy on myself, which I hope I'll never be, and cautious in the face of real danger. What makes me so mad at Greg is simple: I don't think he really knows that difference. And understanding that difference can mean success or failure, life or death.

MAY 3, 1995

Sitting at dinner. Good to be back at Advanced Base Camp and the comfort of an ice-cold rock chair to sit on. Two days of blowing snow forced us out of Camp One. Up there, just below the knife-edge of the ridge, you hear the wind roar over your head, as if you live below subway tracks and the trains never stop coming. Here in ABC we eat quietly, thankful to be in a calm place. "Where's Thor?" Carlo Rocca asks between bites of yak meat. We look at each other, roll our eyes, and shrug.

Good question. Our leader seems to be led. If Kat doesn't want to go to the North Col, Thor doesn't want to go to the North Col. Kat doesn't want to be here. You can tell. She's quiet, looks bored most of the time. Difficult enough to come all this way, eat strange food, suffer through terrible outhouses and cold tents every night when you do want nothing more than to be here. For her, it must be a nightmare. And therefore a nightmare for Thor, who tries to balance our needs for a visible leader against hers—and, I guess, his.

More cracks in the structure: Pat Caffrey had a tough time getting up to Camp One. Takes him three trips to get his equipment up. Then goes back down to ABC, gets lost in a snowstorm, and spends the night bivouacked in some rocks. He's so drained the next day that he takes hours more than he should to get down and develops a respiratory infection.

Then Tony and I got into a childish argument over Thor. The one time I could count on climbing with Thor to Camp Two, Tony insisted on going instead. "Listen, Tony, you've already summited 8,000-meter peaks. Let me go." I needed to have Thor check me out, particularly to see if my pace was too fast. The hell with Tony. I needed some coaching here.

"No. I want to go," Tony fired back, like a little kid who wanted to be with Daddy.

"No way. I'm going," I snarled as I grabbed my backpack and followed Thor out of the tent. Had Tony stamped his feet and sat down and cried, I wouldn't have been surprised. We were both acting like babies. If we're ever going to summit Everest, or even survive this trip safely, we need teamwork, cooperation. Where is it?

Over with the Sherpas, that's where. I find myself spending more time with Motilal, our climbing Sherpa. (Actually he's of the Gurung tribe, not the Sherpa tribe.) Moti speaks English and Japanese fluently, and he is the father figure for all the other Sherpas because he is the oldest, the most experienced. He also has a wife in one valley, another in another valley, a third in the city, and kids everywhere. Moti likes to keep busy. Not bad for a guy who started off as a buffalo boy, a water-buffalo herder. At ABC, Moti is my outrageous alarm clock. He unzips my tent, pulls my sleeping bag out into the cold air, shouting, "Lazy man! You get up!" Later every morning, I visit Moti in his tent—a challenge because he smells so bad. But he keeps me sane up here, the way Emily keeps me sane in Base Camp—both of them friendly, full of fun—a good contrast to the tensions developing. As is Kashi, a young Sherpa so full of fast-moving energy we call him Kami Kashi, after the Japanese kamikaze suicide pilots of World War II.

But, I must admit, all these little cracks in the structure make it difficult to stay confident and positive, especially as we get closer to summit day. Maybe there's some of that kamikaze spirit in all of us.

MAY 5, 1995

Making our way up toward Camp Two is fun; it's a relief from the bickering to be focused on climbing in the steep, hard-packed snow. Today we climb for acclimatization. We intend to get to 25,000 or

26,000 feet, maybe to Camp Two, then return to ABC. Acclimatizing well, breathing easier, legs strong, with Thor ahead of me to keep me at a steady pace, I feel confident climbing to 25,000 feet. Thor turns, smiles back at me, nods his approval. Approval—something I guess I'm still wondering about. I wonder what Roger Gocking thinks, or Russell Brice. Greg and I met Russell and John Tinker, the British climber, at the Asian Trekking office in Kathmandu. No sooner had we met these guys, and without so much as a welcome, they started barking out ground rules: no rescues this year for either of them. (Russell had been to Everest six times and never summited, always hung up on some rescue mission.) Anyone caught stealing would be off the mountain for life. (Last year people were stealing oxygen tanks, masks, even tents.)

They obviously saw us as pretenders, a young kid and a guy with all-new clothes, and they wanted us to know the difference between mountain climbing and 8,000-meter climbing. For Death Zone climbing, you have to have much more stamina and pain tolerance, not to mention the endurance that can keep you going for more than two months. It's not quite the same as eight or nine days of Aconcagua, for example. People like Russell and John have a great dislike of pretenders.

That's why I want to be up here today with Thor—not just to get to Camp Two but to make sure I'm not a pretender. I want to show him I can handle 25,000 feet, that I'm ready for the Death Zone and the summit.

But today I have another problem. One I made myself. Here I am, finally up here with my coach, and everything's going great. But last night I ratted on Thor. Well, not exactly ratted on him. I was talking to my parents—a check-in call—and I mentioned that Thor wasn't spending much time with us. They were going to call Charro, Javier's wife, in Denver, who was going to fax Thor a letter about "my concerns." The problem is the fax will come to the American Base Camp, and people will read it before we get to Advanced Base Camp late this afternoon. Everyone else will know that the fifteen-year-old kid has "concerns" with his expedition leader. I can't say anything about it now because I don't want to spoil a good climb. Talk about communication problems!

The climb goes very well; I learn to pace myself in the steep sections. As we turn back at 25,000 feet and head down to ABC, I see the blue and white of the world above and below me, and feel my legs start to cramp a bit. I know I could handle much more, could have made it to Camp Two, but I'm content that we did so well.

Back at ABC, Thor stands outside the dining tent, studying the piece of paper in his hand, running his fingers through his hair. He is silhouetted by one of those blood-red sunsets gathering its clouds for a dramatic finish to the day. I had wanted to get the fax before he did, but now he has it; now I have to talk to him.

"Didn't think Charro would send the letter." Why do I sound so apologetic? Why do I hate these sorts of conversations?

"I didn't think you had any problems." Thor's serious, formal. "What are they?"

"That you're not climbing enough. I'm worried about my progress, acclimatizing." I hope my voice isn't as shaky as I feel. "Pace." A long pause as we both look out at the sunset. "You gonna climb more—like today?"

"Yeah. I'm climbing more." Thor looks back at the sunset, looks at the paper, and walks away.

Whew! Some confrontation. I hate confrontations. Can't see how some kids can yell at their teachers or referees, or get into fistfights over little things. Man, I can't even "confront" Thor. On one hand, he's my coach and teacher; on the other, I'm paying him and I want my money's worth. Please?

MAY 9, 1995

Ray Dorr and I are on our way to Camp One today, and to the summit the day after tomorrow. I was supposed to summit with Thor. He was to join me at Camp One. I called him on the radio to reconfirm he'd be up the next day—yesterday. Probably should have known— he couldn't make it for two more days. Nothing wrong with that, really. Thor did not have to summit with me or anyone else. As leader, he had to give us direction, advice, but not take us by the hand. (Besides, it was fun to stay alone at Camp One—no one to bother you, eat when you like. I liked it.) Ray and I were both ready, so we hooked up for our summit bid. The American team plans, uses strategies, summits in teams; most expeditions do. We improvise.

Ray and I start from ABC late, around three, to avoid melting snow, falling ice, avalanches. We plan to get to Camp One before dark and get to Camp Three by late afternoon tomorrow. We run into a happy Jim Litch from the American team, who tells us that many of his group have summited and are at Camp One. As we stand there talking, I notice how much Jim is coughing. He speaks maybe a sentence or two, then gets a few mountain hacks out. Then I notice that Ray's doing the same thing. They have a duet of coughs going. Then it finally dawns on me that I'm doing the same thing. All three of us are talking, gulping the thin air, and coughing. And all I notice, respond to, are the words, the conversation. We block out the coughs entirely, both listening to or coughing ourselves. Kind of like having a wind chime in your yard or a grandfather clock—you never notice it after a while. The problem is we all cough up here—most of the time. The air's so thin, the immune system gets so overburdened, we all start coughing.

We leave Jim and get going again. I tell Ray I'm a little tired. He nods, understanding why. I had come down from Camp One late yesterday. Today's my fifth trip up to Camp One—most climbers do only three—and my legs are feeling heavy.

Three-quarters of the way to Camp One, my ordinary mountain hack suddenly turns into a violent storm of coughs. Five, ten coughs, attacking as if there were something inside me wanting out. I'm bent double and feel something let go in my chest; a long, sharp knife slices through my ribs. What is this? I try to straighten up. Can't. Something's holding me bent.

I have to get to Camp One. A doctor for the American team is there. Have to lie down. I start to jumar up a steep section, breathing glass. What is this? The rope, ice covered in the late-day cold, slips, jams the jumar. I stumble up the rope against the pain of the knife in my chest. I can see the tents. The knife slices into me with every move. I pull myself toward the American tent. I see the glow of light, the sound of loud, cheering voices. I can't even take off my pack. What is this? I lurch into the tent. The smiling faces of the summiters greet me.

I seek out the doctor. He pulls up my shirt, pokes around.

"You fractured a rib, I'd say. Been coughing a lot?"

I nod. "Yeah. But I didn't fall or anything."

"You don't have to fall. You cough hard enough, long enough up here, the ribs can't take it."

"Can I rest up? Come up later?"

The doctor shakes his head. "Can't say I recommend it."

I make my way through the crowded tent, feeling like the loser of the Super Bowl in the winners' locker room, careful not to bump any smiling, fist-pumping climbers, congratulating those I know. "Wish you'd been with us. It was great up there!" one exuberant guy yells into my face. I smile weakly back. I can't talk now. It's over for me. No summit. Done. A year's work leaking away in each agonizing breath. Can't think about it right now. Got to get to my tent, get into my sleeping bag, take the codeine pills Ray gave me. Try to sleep. Try not to feel the knife slide in and out of my ribs. Or is it my heart?

MAY 11, 1995

The sun is very warm, reflecting off the snow, as Pemba and I make the long trip down from ABC to Base Camp. I hired Pemba to carry my heavy pack. I carry only a water bottle. We walk slowly, pausing often to drink, to calm the raging fire in my ribs. The disappointment, the frustration, set in yesterday morning when I had to call my parents to tell them, to actually say the words. They sounded relieved, I think; not happy I broke a rib, or happy I'm not going for the summit, just happy I'll be home soon.

Last time down, I was climbing so strongly, mind and legs focused on footwork, efficiency, speed. Now I'm like an old man picking my way down the slope, careful to relieve the pain any way I can, moving slowly enough to pay attention to the mountain in ways I never have. The vast quiet; the magnified texture of light—so bright it almost feels heavy against your body; the feel of the snow; the sculpture of the vistas spread around and below me; the black rock faces, white peaks, and brown valleys all so far away—I'm very lucky to be here on Everest, even though I didn't summit.

I'm lucky, too, to be out of ABC. They should call it ASO for Advanced Soap Opera. It all started when Tony radioed John Tinker, practically begging him to let him use one of the oxygen bottles Tinker had in reserve on the mountain. Tony had summited, taken too much time, and was now out of oxygen. Tinker, annoyed that Tony had not planned well but wanting, above all else, to avoid a rescue, reluctantly agreed. At dusk, Kashi, the Sherpa who accompanied Tony, called, frantic, saying Tony was lost. We kept radios on

On the way to Everest Base Camp

Mount Everest

Everest and Lhotse from summit of Cho Oyu

Jake lounging with a yak

Goofing around with my dad

At rescue and evacuation training in California. It was 138°!

My first ice climb

Ama Dablam team. (Mom is in back row, at left.)

Climbing Ama Dablam

At the summit of Ama Dablam,
with Sherpas Lhakpa and Phurba.
(Everest is in the distance.)

© Ace Kvale

The tiny dots going up Ama
Dablam are actually people.
(I am the third dot from the top.)

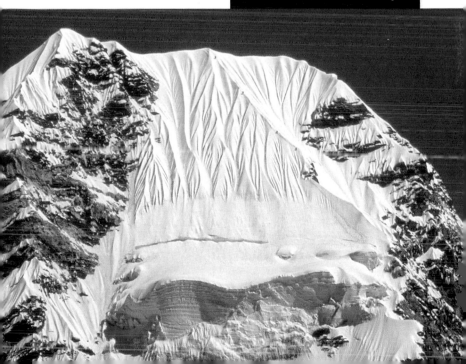

Star trails at Ama Dablam

Scott Fischer's team back at Base Camp

Climbing above Camp Two, my pack weighed 40 pounds!

Crossing a ladder in the Khumbu Icefall

Looking down into a crevasse in the Icefall

Camp Four the morning after the storm. (I stayed in the yellow tent during the storm.)

A climber who has been on Everest since the 1980s

all night at ABC, but not a word from Kashi or Tony. Tinker had to send a rescue team up after all. At five A.M., yesterday, the Sherpa rescue team radioed ABC that they had found Tony. He'd been out all night without a sleeping bag or tent and was almost frozen; he'd be lucky to make it down alive.

Since Jim Wheeler had left, I had become the most qualified EMT, so I became the team "doctor" and got the kitchen tent and medical supplies ready for what would be far worse than a few cracked ribs. Then, later in the morning, came a call from Camp One. Tony's rescuers had brought him into a tent, where, in his gratitude, he was feeling well enough to throw a cup of tea at a Sherpa because it had no sugar. Around three P.M., Tony himself radioed to say he was coming down. Just like that—Tony was back from the dead.

Russell Brice was in our kitchen tent in a flash, followed by John Tinker. Both worked up, both very angry about Tony's need for rescue, telling me Tony would pay big bucks for his irresponsibility, as if I had something to do with it. Tony came stumbling into the kitchen tent around four, looking gray, wasted, weak. He was not welcomed with open arms by anyone. First he claimed he'd spent the night at 28,000 feet—1,000 feet below the summit—without oxygen, contradicting what he had said earlier, on the radio, that he was "coming down with the bottle I slept with." Then he said to me that ESPN and NBC would be after him now. He thought he was a hero.

Tony didn't get it. Nobody else thought that staying out all night at 28,000 feet was a big deal, or the least bit heroic. Not the doctors from other teams who refused to examine him, or the guys from the American team who videotaped his feet so he couldn't claim injury from frostbite, and certainly not Russell and John, who told Tony in very plain language that they had climbing friends all over the world, and if he tried to make himself a hero in any way, he'd be welcome nowhere. Then they hit him with the big bill for Sherpa rescue, Sherpa bonus money, and extra food.

Advanced Soap Opera for me. Real life for professional mountain people like John and Russell. They can't stand "heroes"— phonies who cheapen climbing by acting irresponsibly, have to get rescued from their own stupidity, and then bask in the limelight as if they did something wonderful. What seemed to infuriate Russell and John most was the tea incident. Many men had committed themselves to Tony's rescue, in the dark of night, near the summit of the world's highest mountain. When he rejected tea because it had no sugar, he rejected their efforts, their danger, as just as trivial. John and Russell would not allow that.

Hard to think about such complications as I try to get my sweating old man's body down the steep section into the cooling afternoon shadow, heading for Base Camp, heading for home.

MAY 11, 1995

I'm packing up, then hitching a ride to Kathmandu with the American team. I find out some guy named George called my parents from Base Camp and told them I broke my rib at 26,000 feet. Without checking with me, they told a reporter, who called me when I got down to Base Camp yesterday. In the conversation, the reporter mentioned that I had been higher than I really was. I should have contradicted him right there. But I didn't. To cover my butt, I said I'd been to Camp Two, because that's at 26,000 feet. But I lied. I only got to 25,000 feet. It really bothered me all night. I kept thinking about it. I didn't mean to lie; it just seemed to happen. Bad enough I had a rib gnawing at me with every breath; now I had a lie festering around inside my head. I don't know which was worse, but

I do know lying was a stupid thing to do. Lie? For what? I didn't want to be a Tony. I wasn't trying to be a hero. I couldn't make the rib get better any faster, but I did know what to do about the lie. I called the guy early the next morning, told him about the mix-up and that I lied to cover up the mix-up. He was very good about it. When we hung up, my head felt a lot better. He never even mentioned it in the article. Nobody knew but me.

As I pack up, people come by my tent to say good-bye. Greg Miller wants to leave with us, but there's not enough room. He topped out at Camp Two. He wanted so badly to make it, he even wanted to hire Reinhardt Patscheider to get him to the summit. Reinhardt was a little tired. He had returned from Kathmandu feeling better and decided to summit solo. He summited by the light of the moon, so strong, up and down so fast, we wondered who the guy in bright yellow was coming down to ABC at dawn.

Pat Caffrey presents me with a plaque for my "attempted summit." He never got high up because of altitude and respiratory problems. Carlo Rocca ran out of gas. Maybe things would have been different with a personal Sherpa. Carlo's in great shape for a sixty-three-year-old triple-bypass survivor. But the oldest guy who ever summited Everest was Dick Bass, fifty-five. I wonder now that I'm leaving if Thor thought enough about the publicity value of the youngest kid and the oldest man trying to summit on the same expedition team. Imagine how he'd look to the climbing world if both of us had made it!

Not many of our team made it. In fact, only one did. Roger and Moti ran into terrible weather and turned back with 1,500 feet to go. Ray got caught up in Tony's rescue, and didn't have the proper gear with him for a summit bid. Kat and Thor made it to Camp Three. As it turns out, the only climber on our team to summit is Tony. And I'm about to get on a truck with a team that had every member on the summit.

MAY 12, 1995

We're on a bouncing truck, heading for the Freedom Bridge. For some reason, curling down muddy mountain roads in an old truck with huge drop-offs, rockfalls, and washouts is far more unnerving than climbing down from Camp One. Frequently, washouts force us to abandon our vehicles to cross the ravaged sections of road on foot. Then we transfer all our equipment into other trucks, which take us to the next washout. By far, my most dangerous bit of climbing the whole trip is stumbling 50 feet across a washout with my rib throbbing, water splashing down the muddy crevasses in the road, slipping under the weight of heavy duffels, fighting off Tibetan porters grabbing at your stuff so they'll get paid, and the whole scene on such a treacherous area that the Russian climbers on the truck ahead of us have fixed ropes to get across safely. It's like the classic nightmare: you're slipping away toward the abyss; far below are little trees and dots of animals. There's too much pushing and shoving on the slippery mud. You feel your balance going, going, goooone!

Later, in Nepal, we go through a hot little village. Everything is so green. I didn't realize how much my eyes hungered for green. It all looks so wonderful. Trees. Grass. Plants. And a little river. With kids swimming. Someone yells to the driver to stop. We all jump out of the truck and, to the amazed looks of the kids, take off our shoes and shirts and jump in with them. The water is warm, the trees are green, the kids laugh, and so do we.

MAY 13, 1995

Kathmandu. I roll over in bed, rib still killing me, reminding me every minute that I didn't make it; the thoughts stabbing my every breath. I feel devastated one minute because I didn't summit, then happy the next because I'm going home. Then awful the next because I let so many people down, then great because I climbed so high up on Everest. Did I prepare well enough? What do I tell all those people who wished me luck? All those who sponsored me? How much I've learned, for one thing. How I had great fear of going over 25,000 feet—it's as if someone has turned the oxygen off up there, and you just shrivel up and die a little with each breath. Now I feel that I can exist up there as well as anyone. I have a lot of beta on the mountain now—a lot of information.

I know one thing: I'm glad I came here. Happy my parents and so many others are supporting me in so many ways. I could be sitting in my tenth-grade English class right now in my little town in Rhode Island. I'd rather be alone in Kathmandu, sleepless, tossing around in pain from a broken rib. It's funny with goals, though: the higher you want to go, the higher you do go. When I started a trek last year, I never saw this moment in my future. Most of the kids sitting in that English class never even think of getting a passport— never think they'll use one. But almost every one of them could do what I'm doing or something like it.

At the risk of sounding too corny, or making a big deal of myself, I'd like to get up in front of those kids, show them my passport (which is full of stamps from so many countries), then hand out passport applications. I wonder how many would fill them out? How many could expand their dreams and their vision of themselves to imagine their passports filled, too? They can do it. I have the passport and broken rib to prove it.

my mother's necklace

OCTOBER 14, 1995

I'm in the Himalayas, sitting on a stool in Base Camp doing geometry problems, and looking up at the summit of Ama Dablam. We're maybe five miles away from Everest, although it's hard to tell distances in this sea of mountains. I try to do another problem, but I'm distracted by the mountain and stare up at its summit, 22,350 feet up. I feel as a small ant must feel in front of a huge, wide building— intimidated to a degree, but itching to get climbing. It's called Ama Dablam because from its summit hangs a long, steep snowfield shaped like a *dablam*, a pendant or ornament, hanging from a mother's necklace. Ama Dablam, or "mother's necklace" in English, is a classic Himalayan peak: challenging, steep, and beautiful. I'm very lucky to be here.

Coming off Everest, I saw Al Burgess in Kathmandu; he invited me to join his expedition and here I am, rib healed, ready for more climbing. So why am I doing geometry problems? My usual answer is Mr. Krupowicz, the assistant superintendent, who always gets permission for me to miss school as long as I make up my work. I always try to get to the work at some point or other. But the specific reason I'm sitting here, on this beautiful morning, doing geometry is my mother. She's making me do it. She won't let me off the stool until I've done twenty problems. And she can make sure I've done all twenty, because she's here! In Base Camp.

My mom decided she wanted to come and got ready for the long trek by walking five miles a day at home. Now she is here, doing very well. My father prefers to "keep the home fires burning," as he says. He already had his life of adventure in nineteen years of late-night shifts as a police officer. When I look in his scrapbook of articles and pictures, I see him standing in the uniformed line—trim, tall, squinting into the camera, ready to take on the world. I see stories commemorating him for diving into Narragansett Bay to save a fifteen-year-old girl from a submerged car, or of him disarming a man bent on using a shotgun to blow away a bar full of people. The nineteen years of sleep deprivation took its toll. The sleep expert said he'd never heard of anyone lasting beyond four years of third shift. Dad lasted nineteen on two, three hours of sleep each day. He wanted to be able to see my sister and me, so he gave up a chance at the three-to-eleven shift, knowing we'd always be in school when he was at home, at home when he was at work. Eventually, the sleep deprivation forced him to retire. No wonder he likes the order and comfort of home.

How do I feel about my mom being here? How would any fifteen-year-old guy feel about taking his mother along when he's out with his friends on an incredible adventure? Especially when she's nagging me to do homework, and my sit-ups, and to brush my teeth? Actually, I like her being here. We get along well, play backgammon every night, talk. And it's fun watching her go through the experience of Nepal.

Picture an energetic little American lady with short gray hair shopping in the madhouse of the marketplace in Namche Bazaar for the first time. Watch her try to negotiate prices with the sellers. A pair of handmade, yak-wool socks for 150 rupees (about $2.95); a coral necklace for 350 rupees; a sunstone necklace, another 350 rupees; a carving, chain, and pendant for 150 rupees; all light, little things. That's my mom! Probably paid much more than any Nepali would, but so what—it's still very inexpensive. As was the hotel in Namche Bazaar. Three nights, three meals a day for the two of us: $55. Proudly displaying her treasures to me, Mom held her chain and pendant in front of me and said, "Got my *dablam*, now you have to get yours."

Then she scared the hell out of me hiking up here to Base Camp. I was ahead of her, almost up to 16,000 feet by now, with the trail having sloped steeply uphill, and had been for a good five hours or so. I could usually keep an eye on her in the distance behind me. I got to the top of the ridge, where I could see the whole trail clearly below me. I spotted Mom's jacket on the ground almost 2,000 feet below, and my mother in it! Stretched out! Dead? I didn't know. I ran all the way down, screaming, "Mom! Mom!" She didn't move. Heart attack? Poison food? She never should have come.

As I came up to her, she jumped up, saying *I* had scared the hell out of *her*! She said she had fallen asleep. "Listen to your body, you said. So I did. My body said to go to sleep. So I lay down." I had her dead, and all she did was take a snooze.

My mom's adjusted pretty well to life in a Himalayan Base Camp. And she's pretty cheerful about it all. But she also has a tough time with stuff I hardly ever notice anymore. I can tell because she keeps talking about things like showers, clean hair, her bed at home, riding in a car, American food—as if she'll never have them again. And she's taking it out on me with geometry! "Do your homework! You promised Mr. Krupowicz you'd do it. And you're not going to move until you finish all twenty problems!"

Why did I let her come? I'm the only person in the history of Himalayan climbing stuck doing geometry homework. Could be worse. I could be stuck on a beautiful day like this doing these same problems in a study hall at Middletown High School, instead of here in the best base camp in the Himalayas, maybe the world. We're on a grassy meadow, sheltered from wind, with a clear stream of water running through and Ama Dablam as our backdrop. The sort of base camp that'll spoil you, the sort of place, if it were back in the States, that'd be overrun with RV hookups, people watching TV, and the smell of hundreds of hamburgers on grilles. Not that Base Camp is deserted. Must be 150 people here. But out here it's just so clean and quiet and restful, it's hard to leave.

My mother's over near her tent talking, waiting for me to finish these geometry problems, and I have to admit I'm getting really steamed. She's talking to Al and Travis Spitzer, the leaders of our expedition, who are on the way up to Camp Two to fix ropes. Why didn't they ask me to come? I'm tired of commercial expeditions. I'm sick of being a passenger, like some little old lady on a guided tour—might as well put me on a bus and tell me where to get off to look at the next castle the way old ladies do in Europe. This morning, I told my mother that I'm ready to climb on my own. Big mistake. "You'll do exactly what Al says to do. He's got thirty-three years' experience, and he's still here to talk about it!" Then she said I better have a major attitude change. Then, instead of the original ten geometry problems, she raised it to twenty.

As I sit here wrestling with geometry, I start thinking she's right. Do what Al says. Otherwise I might not be as lucky as I was in August. I had met Chris Fowler, a sportscaster at ESPN, at the Extreme Games in Newport near my home. Chris, his brother, Drew, and I decided to climb Mount Rainier in Washington, a 14,400-foot peak, the most glaciated in the continental United States.

We were climbing on the glacier toward the summit when I noticed a small depression in the snow. Instinct told me to test the area with my ice ax. The ax went right through the ice, exposing a foot-wide hole through which I could see into a deep crevasse. Looking for solid ice, I stabbed the ax into the ice to the left of us. It went through. To the right. Through again. We were standing on a very thin layer of ice and snow, an ice bridge, with nothing below the three of us but hundreds of feet of open crevasse! If we went down, we'd never be found.

I remembered my experience on that snow cornice at NOLS last year, and how I fought down the panic rising in my throat. I knew we'd be OK if we stayed calm, rational. And we were. Careful to stay in our exact footsteps, we slowly went back down the way we'd come up, eventually making it to solid ice, where we sat for some time, sipping water, slowly gaining back our composure.

What kept preying on my mind, walking on the beach a few days later in Oregon, was the horrible, helpless, empty feeling of my ice ax breaking through the glacier. We had summited successfully, had a great time in Oregon and Vancouver, but that feeling of the ice ax hitting air stayed with me every night, reminding me how close I had been to death. Then, when I returned to Rhode Island, I learned about the deaths of two young climbers. Sean, a guide on Rainier, fell while attempting a rescue. Alison Hargreaves, the first woman to summit Everest solo without oxygen, had died on K2 with five others. I knew both. Sean was a friendly twenty-year-old I had met in a camp on Rainier just a week before. Alison's tent was near mine on Everest, so we talked often.

I can still see Alison, Sean, the ice ax plunging through, and know how close I came to joining them. None of these thoughts will ever scare me off the mountains. Not that I won't be scared; I'll be scared plenty of times. But thoughts of Alison and Sean do serve as signs—big, red, neon signs—to be careful of every step on every climb.

So OK, I will listen to Al, Mom. I will do what he says. And not just to get out of more geometry.

OCTOBER 15, 1995

On the way to Camp Two. I'm waiting for Al to get off rope so I can get around the corner and up a narrow ledge. Al finally yells down that he's off—I can't see him from down here—but I know I had to wait. Nothing worse than two guys yanking on a rope from two directions when you have to jumar up a steep section. This is steep. And scary. We're on a rock face that's about vertical. And on the rock face, there is a ledge that you have to scoot across sideways, then get up on top of the ledge and over the rock face.

What gets scary is you are on a face that is 5,000 feet straight down. I clip onto the rope and start to work my way across the ledge. I have to twist one leg against the rock face, squish around for a handhold, then swing my body out, leaning into the side of the rock so I can get my two feet balanced on little nubs of rock. I can only look down at my feet and, consequently, down to the reddish-brown valley far below. Rock climbers do this stuff all the time. I've done it myself, but there are some big differences. Like the twenty-five-pound backpack I'm carrying, which gets stuck in the gap in the rock face. Like the incredible feeling of height on the razor-thin ledge on this vertical ridge of Ama Dablam. Like the feelings of panic I have to fight with all my energy.

I am not fearless; no climber is. What I try to do is control the panic. I dread this ledge at the same time that I love being here. But I must control the panic. I must resist a beginner's climbing mind.

No thoughts of *Oh no, oh no, oh no.* No thoughts of *I'm stuck, can't go forward, can't go back.* Otherwise I might freeze up like a statue. I stay calm. I stay positive. I take my time and fight the thoughts of *I could die—right now.* Panic has a lot to do with accidents in the mountains, so the ability to fight anxiety and nervousness is very important. One way I do it is to develop a great sense of trust in my equipment. I have to believe the pitons and ropes will be there, will hold me up. It's a little like rappelling. You have to trust that first step over the edge, when you feel for a split second as if you are in free-fall. Have to believe that you'll be OK. If I fall from this ledge, 5,000 feet up, I have to relax, because I know from the few times I slipped rappelling that I'll fall only as far as the rope will allow. Not that it's easy to think about when you're dependent on a few hooks and a skinny rope and all you can see below your feet are rocks 5,000 feet down.

I wiggle, scratch, and shimmy my way to the top. What a heart-pounding rush! The sort of complicated climbing that makes Ama Dablam such a classic mountain. There are more difficult spots in many mountains, but it's a thrill to get through this. All seven team members do: Travis; then Al; then me; followed by Ace Kvale, an adventure photographer from Colorado; Anne Smith, Ace's girl-friend; Allison Palmer, a physical therapist from England; and Bob Mante, an engineer from Tucson. Aside from Bob, a weekend desert-mountain climber, I'm the least experienced, which is fine with me. That means that every time I can get through this ledge, and the dread/love coming back down, I'll gain more confidence in myself and my team.

OCTOBER 16, 1995

You never know where you're going to have an adventure. Phurba, a Sherpa, and I are sitting on a rock at Camp One with a book. I am helping him with his English, but we are lazily distracted by the panorama available to the eye at Camp One—a long ledge populated with the tents of many expeditions. Behind us is a pile of rocks angled steeply to a snowfield. Below, we look down thousands of feet to clouds, red earth, snow, green valleys, and tiny birds riding the thermals. Phurba loves to learn English, and I am very relaxed after this day's climb to Camp Two. We joke about my Nepali and his English.

Now for the adventure part. Above us, maybe a hundred yards, a woman is coming down through the rocks. She's a member of the Spanish team; I can tell by her jacket. She stumbles, unleashing a flurry of small boulders, which tumble straight for Phurba and me. I feel just like a human bowling pin! A strike by these bouncing boulders could crush a tent or our skulls. If a tent gets it, all our equipment gets it—expedition over. If I get it, I won't need the tent's equipment anyway. A teacher told me before I left for this trip how different I was from most kids my age. He said I'm one teenager he met who didn't think he was indestructible. Now, as the beachball-sized boulders stampede toward us, I think I know what he meant.

The woman is screaming, "Sorry! Careful!" then something in Spanish. The rocks are growling, picking up speed. Twenty-five yards away now. I try to pick one to avoid, but there are five or six, all on ever-changing courses. I could jump out of one's path right into the path of another. I'm bouncing on my feet, ready to go one way or the other, the growl louder, the boulders close enough to read! Nowhere to go, Phurba and I stand ready to accept our fates like two bullfighters ready for the charge.

Then it's over. An upswell of rock catches all six boulders ten yards short of the tents. The bowling balls lose their momentum. A fine dust sprinkles over our heads, the woman pulls her hands from her eyes and waves an apology, Phurba picks up his book, and we settle down once again to the quiet vista and the study of English.

OCTOBER 19, 1995

Summit day, Camp Three. An icy wind. Since Ace, Anne, and Allison had to give up yesterday because of the cold, the worst Al's ever seen here, we start late, hoping for a little sun warmth. Travis, then me, followed by Bob, Phurba, and Lhakpa, another Sherpa. Al had begun again this morning before us but had to return to camp to warm his hands. He says its at least 30 below, with windchill—the sort of cold that tears at your throat. The two Sherpas have only one pair of heavy gloves between them, but that will not keep them from a summit bid. Their love of the mountains is too strong. Besides, it's a territorial thing. Not many Nepali guys from outside the Khumbu Valley come in and climb here, so they can't wait to strut their stuff for the hometown boys.

We start up next to the *dablam*, a steep snow and ice field, and in the wind I hear yelling in Nepali. I look back and there's Al, already caught up to us, yelling at one of the Sherpas, who's stuck in the classic can't-go-up, can't-go-down freeze you never want to be in. Al screams at him as if he's a stubborn yak, and slowly Phurba thaws out enough to continue up the *dablam*. As cold as it is, we make good progress up the hard snowpack, inching toward the summit: Travis, me, Al, Bob, Phurba, and Lhakpa (who trade gloves back and forth, keeping one hand in a pocket at all times).

Soon I'm standing alone on a portion of the summit the size of a Volkswagen-bug roof. The wind knocks me around so much I sit down, legs exhausted, and look down behind me into the amazingly sheer 10,000-foot drop of Ama Dablam's North Face, then across to Everest's South Face, where, right now, there are teams crawling up to the summit. The huge snow plume tells me the wind is even stronger there than here. I am content to be summiting here on Ama Dablam, my highest Himalayan peak. I am the youngest ever to summit here. I don't pump my arms, or dance, or even declare victory. I sit alone, the warm, golden rush coursing through my head and body, and look out over a sea of mountains, snow-covered peaks off in the distance like whitecaps on the Atlantic near my home. On very clear days like this, some from Everest have claimed to see the curvature of the earth; others say they can see the Indian Ocean, hundreds of miles away. I know I'm looking out over 150, 200 miles at least, and it makes me feel very small—a little dot on the top of a cold, windswept mountain, waiting for three other climbers to join me. Bob comes up, gets video of the two of us, then tapes Phurba and Lhakpa, grinning like little kids. After ten minutes, we start down.

Coming down is a question of balance. The ropes are very thin up here (who wants to carry up 300 pounds of thick rope?), demanding that your legs take much of your weight, setting your thighs into screaming fits. Worse than leg cramps for me is Accutane. I developed a cystic acne problem on Everest—the type of acne that causes eruptions under your skin, making your face look like pepperoni pizza. The dermatologist gave me Accutane, told me not to do any sports in the sun. Now I know why. High-altitude sun and a high dosage of vitamin A are swelling my joints, blurring my vision, infecting my fingernails, cracking my lips, making me a mess. I have to admit it's all my fault. Should have listened to the doctor. Or at least not taken the Accutane. But I'm not going to stop climbing, and there are too many good-looking girls out there to go around with a pizza face if I can avoid it. So I suffer.

Travis takes one look at me and insists he stay with me in Camp Three. I can cook, melt water, take care of myself, don't need a twenty-four-year-old guy taking care of me. But Travis won't go. For our summit celebration, we cook the worst-tasting ramen noodles with garlic and onions—then, even worse, mix peach Tang in the water we cook it in for our drinks. I'd almost rather get a headache from dehydration than drink peach Tang with bits of garlic and onion floating around.

OCTOBER 20, 1995

I meet a climber in a bright orange jacket coming up—too late, I think, to be going for the summit and back to Camp Three before dark. We talk; he's actually going for the summit and back to Base Camp, not Camp Three—before dark. He turns to go up the trail, and I pause on a rock below him, turning to find him taking my picture. It's Peter Habeler, according to a climber I meet later at Camp Two, one of the world's best high-altitude climbers. He summited Everest with Reinhold Messner, without oxygen, in 1974. (I'd love to have that photo: me on a rock on Ama Dablam, taken by Peter Habeler, a guy I've read so much about.) I'm almost down to Camp One, thinking about the picture, and *whoosh*, the orange jacket catches up to me, goes by me again, says hello, and is gone, doing sixty in a thirty-mile-per-hour zone.

When I get down to Base Camp, I find my mom waiting for me in a confusion of emotions. Yes, she's happy I made it in one piece. But, she wants to know, what happened to my face? After her, Habeler's one of the first people I see. He's as calm and fresh as if he'd been sitting around Base Camp all day instead of gliding through a climb in a matter of hours—a climb that took me two days to stumble through. He ignores my red, raw face and bleeding lips and congratulates me. Commends me on my pace. Says he's glad to see me take my time. Older guys like him get too complacent, and that's when people get hurt. He smiles, wishes me a long future in climbing.

OCTOBER 23, 1995

Last day in Base Camp. Tomorrow we leave for home. A group of us spend the morning talking about the possibilities of going to Everest next spring. Funny to sit here in this beautiful base camp, looking at Everest rising so peacefully in the distance and making plans once again to stand at its peak. Everest is not that far away, either in distance or in time. Only four months to get sponsors, to train, to make specific plans. By March, I'll be here again. I know I will.

We pose for our group photo. Everyone is laughing and relaxed. Ace, Allison, and Anne are ready for another summit bid tomorrow in much warmer weather. Mom and I will head back to Lukla, then Kathmandu, Bangladesh, Singapore, Amsterdam, and New York. Tonight we have a special chocolate cake that Kheddar, our cook, made. And later, we'll be outside trying to get photos of meteors and stars over Ama Dablam. Hope some come out.

Meanwhile, it's wonderful just to stand here huddled together for this picture: a great group of people who worked so well together. I look over at my mom, smiling and tanned, so proud to have survived the hardships of a mountain base camp so well. Around her neck, I see the necklace she bargained for in Namche Bazaar. I can see the *dablam* hanging down from the chain. She won her necklace and I won mine. I look up at the summit and I smile. I've been there. Done that.

CHAPTER TWELVE to base camp with cameras

I'm watching *Rocky V*. Rocky Balboa's blood is flying all over the place as he goes down again when a bright light flashes in my face, and a video camera works its way up to my seat and watches me watching Rocky Balboa fight. People all around me are trying to sleep, or watch the movie, or read, until the bright light breaks into their quiet. We are out over the Pacific, eight hours into a thirteen-hour flight, the first leg of my trip to Everest, a funny place to have a video camera stuck in my face.

I can't complain about the camera. I encouraged it. It was a business decision. I've spent a lot of time on the phone over the last few months trying to get sponsors—companies or people who will help pay my expenses. Every day, making sponsor calls became as much a part of preparation for Everest as 1,000-rep workouts, and as important. Without sponsor help, I'd still be home.

Sponsors love publicity. After all, that's why they sponsor me, or anyone else—so people will see their products toughing it out on

Everest. If sponsors get more publicity through me, then they'll give me more support for the next trip—more money, more equipment. Right now I'm completely sponsored: Tag Heuer (watches), Power-Bar (nutritional snacks), Uvex (sunglasses), Black Diamond (technical equipment), Gregory (backpacks), Polarmax (long underwear), and Globe Manufacturing. And I'm on a low-budget trip—about $24,000. Most trips to the south, or Nepal, side of Everest cost over $30,000; some as high as $65,000. So every opportunity to raise money through exposure and publicity becomes very important.

A New York producer called about two months ago, wanting to film my Everest trip and try to interest National Geographic for a special. Can't miss, he said. He'd have a film crew follow me from L.A. to Nepal to Base Camp, then I'd film up the mountain.

A National Geographic Special on me! I told him I had to think about it. Sounds silly. To have to think about being the focus of a national TV special following my trip to break a world record. Anyone would jump at the chance, right? I had to think about it.

I don't climb for publicity. I never once called a newspaper or TV station. I always feel strange being interviewed; I'll put off meetings as if they were dentist appointments. I'd rather just go climb without any publicity at all. I realize that people are interested, that publicity can help me in the future, that I should take advantage of the opportunity. But I still have trouble dealing with it.

First, that AP story went out about me wanting to climb Everest last year when I was fifteen, and Sir Edmund Hillary opposed my attempt. Even all the publicity in between seemed to be crazy. *CBS This Morning*, *NBC Nightly News*, newspaper articles—I didn't look for any of it, particularly the stories that criticized and questioned my parents for allowing me to go to Everest. With all the publicity, there always seemed to be a negative, a darker shade to any story I saw about me and my parents.

After all my preparation for Everest—climbing in Peru, Argentina, Ecuador, and last year's Everest climb in Tibet, all the 1,000-rep workouts, and running hospital stairs, all the expenses and hopes—it came down to publicity, to a video camera. And the more I thought about it, the more I knew I'd cooperate, because I knew I wanted to climb 8,000-meter peaks again, and sponsors don't give money to some young kid no one's ever heard of.

If you've ever had a camera on you for any length of time, you smile, look "on," "act" for about ten minutes, then you kind of forget about it. You can't be "on" forever, so you just start to act normal. Well, normal for me on this plane trip is acting like a commuter. This is my third trip to Nepal in three years, so what was exciting the first time is now pretty ordinary. If these guys had filmed me two years ago, they would have had a smiling kid, happy to have a movie, food, and a pillow. What they get now is the blank face of a confined, counting-the-hours traveler.

Roles seem to get reversed. I'm the calm traveler; the camera crew, all sophisticated New Yorkers, are the ones who act like kids. When we stop in Korea, the police warn the crew not to use cameras in the airport. They film me anyway. During the twelve-hour stop in Thailand, I've learned never to leave the airport in Bangkok, to head for an airport day room to sleep, to eat nothing but chocolate bars until we're back in flight. The crew goes into downtown Bangkok, a place much scarier than Everest will ever be, and just about makes it back in time for our flight, looking exhausted but excited by their twelve hours of play in Bangkok.

Forty hours after leaving L.A., we land in Kathmandu, and I run for customs—a trick I've learned to get through more quickly. The crew is on my tail, but I tell them no filming; they'd lose their cameras to these Nepali police in no time—as if they were going to take away the secret to Nepali life with their cameras.

I've learned to avoid downtown Kathmandu. Climbers who spend time roaming around the city take a very big risk of getting sick and never even getting to the mountain, so the crew gets little footage. Jabion, my Sherpa buddy, is another story. Imagine meeting a good friend for the first time in months. Then imagine you can't talk to him until the camera's ready. And when it is ready, you finally get to talk and laugh and say hello—six times, pretending that each one is the first. Jabion, smiling as ever, looks very confused after the third or fourth time he thanks me for getting him on this trip.

MARCH 28, 1996

Our first team meeting and dinner in our hotel. First there's Brigeete, the Belgian climber and guide, married to John Muir, a Scotsman crazy enough to cross the Australian desert dragging a cart with forty days' worth of water. She's stocky, with blond, sun-streaked hair, about thirty-three, a strong, intelligent climber who's been on Everest before. Then there's Ray Dorr. I know him well from Everest '95. Paul Deegan's a tall, lanky outdoors instructor for the British Royal Air Force. His buddy, Neil Laughton, is also in the British military, a wiry thirty-year-old who's as quiet as Paul is funny. Graham Ratcliffe is also from England. He's in his forties, married with two kids, an auto mechanic who summited the north side of Everest last year. All of these people are experienced in high altitude; most know Henry Todd, our leader, well and immediately give me a sense of confidence.

Finally, there's Thomas and Tina from Sweden, both blond, about forty, who made their money delivering toilet paper, who trained for Everest by doing karate four hours a day, and who had altitude sickness on Mount McKinley at 20,000. Henry had told me about them, how he needed to fill out the team, how otherwise it would cost us all that much more. We can only hope—I keep my fingers crossed—that they will have great inner strength. Missing is Michael Jorgesen of Denmark. He'll join us in Base Camp.

APRIL 12, 1996

Two weeks of hiking gets us close to Base Camp. Same type of nine-hundred-year-old trail that I trekked with Al when I was fourteen. That seems so long ago, when I was a young kid. But this time I'm very strong, move along at my own pace, comfortable with or without company, finding my way to the teahouses we stay at each night in ancient little villages like Lukla, Pangboche, Namche Bazaar, Dingboche; all the time ascending higher and higher into the Himalayas and acclimatizing to the altitude. We travel fast enough to make four or five miles a day, which is also slow enough to acclimatize naturally and walk the old trail where I sometimes smell the same plant life as I did on Ama Dablam. The bright sunshine and clear nights meld one day into the next, until we can see Everest so close it seems we'll be there any minute. Then we hike ten more miles, and it still seems exactly the same distance away.

The video camera is becoming like that albatross, and I'm the Ancient Mariner. Every time I think I want to get a good shot, I have to decide if I want to get a still for sponsors or slide shows or video footage for the documentary. Say there are some kids playing in a little square in Namche Bazaar, and the smiles show the great fun they're having, despite their dirty faces and ragged clothes; or I see a beautiful bird against a white cliff of snow, or the furls of colorful flags against the deep blue sky. Do I snap a few photos? Take the time to get out the video camera? If I hesitate, I'll lose the whole thing. If I take one, I lose the other.

I know. It's my own fault for agreeing to videotape, but I never thought it would be so much work. It's another part-time job to do.

The flip side of video is being in it. The crew wants me to do everything twice or three times. One morning I had to do six takes, just coming out the door of the Rhododendron Lodge in Deboche. Finally I just left, fast, to get on the trail. To be by myself.

How about a video journal? That's what the producer, Jeff Swimmer, asked me to do after he and his crew finally left. I set up the camera on a tripod, clip a mike to my shirt, and just talk. I have a whole list of questions about what I do each day, about how I get along with Henry Todd and the other climbers. I'm not going to tell the camera about all our arguing, or that Thomas and Tina are from another planet, or that Henry sometimes is very impatient. If I run out of things to say, I'm to talk about my future goal—being an emergency-room doctor—or compare myself physically and mentally to last year—much stronger, much more confident.

I try to smile and be a good TV person and talk to the camera as if it were a friend, but after hiking six or seven hours in the thin air, I know I'm kind of dull. Most kids would jump at this chance. Ever see the people outside the *Today* show or at games, waving "Look at me"? For me, it's different. Like the time I called home before I got the helicopter for Lukla. Last time I'll talk to my parents for a month, and there's Jeff and the all-seeing eye right in my face.

I'm trying to talk, and the camera's waiting for me to cry or say something profound so it can show millions of people what that kid said to his mother just before he went to Everest. I keep turning away from the camera. I am homesick, I'll admit, and I have a long way to go before I get home, but I'm not going to show the camera that! No way. I smile and talk as if I'm down the street and I'll be home in time for dinner.

Another highlight: yak herding. One morning, I can't wait to get going. The rest of the team is slow to get organized. I see the trail, and a warm morning, and my goal of getting to the Japanese Memorial by noon all going down the tube, so I take off. I get half a mile and run into a string of yaks carrying equipment for Rob Hall's Adventure Consultants team to Base Camp, and I know I'm done. Yaks, just to remind you, are like cows with long hair. Female yaks are naks. Yaks and naks don't live well below 9,000 feet. Dzos and dzoms—male and female crossbreeds of yaks and cattle—are like yaks and naks, but are comfortable at sea level. There are, by the way, many more dzos and dzoms than there are yaks and naks, in case you wondered. And most of them are fairly quiet. Just watch out for the nasty ones with the rings in their noses and the huge, wild ones that sometimes roam the upper mountains in Tibet.

Take thirty yaks in single file loaded down with wide boxes. Put them on a trail that's sometimes so narrow you can touch the high stone walls on either side with your outstretched arms. Have them plod along at yak speed, and you have a Himalayan traffic jam. Hurry all you want; it won't matter to the yaks. Hit them with stones, scream at them (which the herders do all day long); nothing moves them any faster than slow-motion, yak pace. Try to pass them and you'll be smooshed against the side of the rocks, or get your foot stomped on, or you'll be nudged over the edge of a cliff. They're like the tide, which never stops, never changes. And I'm stuck behind them.

So I become a yak herder. Nowhere to go, nothing else to do. I throw rocks at yak butts and try to imitate the yak herders' high-pitched yells, both of which the yaks completely ignore, and I walk in yak dung and smell the yak stink for hour after hour.

The other herders look at me as if I'm crazy. They're dressed in grimy ragged coats and spend their days (months, years, lives) herding loaded yaks up and down the trails of the Khumbu Valley, yelling and throwing stones at yak horns and butts, keeping them moving, exactly as their fathers and grandfathers and ancestors have done for centuries. Nothing but yak speed, all day, every day. Stop screeching at them, stop pelting them with rocks, and they'll stop dead. Imagine a string of thirty yaks just standing there, blocking up the trail for miles, and it's all your fault! So you never let that happen. You just keep on yelling and throwing rocks and moving through your whole life at yak speed.

The yak herders don't know what to make of me. I'm clean, dressed in clothes they could never afford, an American kid, herding the yaks. *Why?* they must think. Here they are, doing the lowest form of work Sherpas do, always stepping in yak crap, with nothing more than a bowl of rice and a ratty blanket for comfort, and here I come in my new climber's clothes and backpack, herding the yaks for fun? We never talk. Just yell and throw rocks: keep the tide moving.

Finally we come to a wide part of the trail. I put it in passing gear and go past all thirty of them like a shot. Soon the yak bells are tinkling in the distance and I'm moving at Mark speed, not yak speed.

Yet another highlight: Meet Jake, a trekker who came all the way to Base Camp with us. He's sixteen, quit school to hike (with his mother, no less), wears baggy pants, has weird taste in music, and disagrees with me on just about everything we talk about.

But we have a great time together, mainly just screwing around. We're crossing a rickety bridge one day—the kind that's over a hundred feet above a quiet river but has so many holes punched in its wooden roadway by yaks that you have to watch every step. It's after-lunch quiet just outside a village. Jake struggles toward me, as if he's carrying a dead body. When he gets closer, I see it's a large stone. He struggles and gets it up to the railing, where he hesitates, gives me a malicious look, and sends the stone plummeting with a huge, very loud splash. He giggles like a madman, and I'm panicked we'll get thrown out of town for causing so much noise.

The next night, he's all set to zip the film crew into their tent for the night. So what, you might say. Worse things have happened. Not to the film crew. They're all sick. It doesn't take much in a third-world country—a Coke drunk from a glass, some drops of water, and before you know it you wish you could set up your bed in a nice clean bathroom, because you'll be spending a lot of quality time on that toilet. So Jake's idea—heh, heh, heh—is to zip these four sick guys into their tent. See how things come out in the morning. Heh, heh, heh. Fortunately for them, it's too cold for us to get out of bed.

Typical teenage stuff.

In one small town, three Sherpa girls about our age start flirting with us. I hand them pictures of my family and my dogs. I ask for the pictures back; they smile and take off with the pictures. We chase them down one alley, up another. They run easily in the altitude. We're huffing like two old men. Every time we get close, they just laugh and run away. They come just close enough for us to grab their scarves. They're very good-looking girls, but they are, shall we say, unwashed. In fact, they smell. Strongly. In fact, their faces and hands are very dirty. Jake and I take the scarves, and the girls sit on a rock near the teahouse, waiting for us to do something. Jabion comes along, sees the scarves, smiles at us, and says, "Congratulations. You are in love."

"Love?" I ask. "What do you mean, love?"

"When you take scarves—sign of love in Nepal." The girls look at us from their rock, waiting as if for something good to happen to their lives. "Maybe you marry them?"

Jake and I throw the scarves into the air and, before they can land, we've grabbed our backpacks and are down the trail, with the girls' giggly voices echoing in the distance: "Come back. Come back."

APRIL 17, 1996

Base Camp is crazy, a carnival of colorful tents and flags, a small city of about three hundred from the United States, New Zealand, Taiwan, Sweden, Scotland, South Africa, Spain, Russia, and England—a small city where there is no organization, no central control of anything, no streets, not even trees or grass or even ground; just a sea of brightly colored tents, erected on a pile of rocks on top of a glacier. Which melts and moves. So climbers coming down from the mountain sometimes find their tents at odd angles. At night you can hear the roar of the river of melted snow coursing through the glacier beneath your ear, and you swear it's an inch away. The place feels alive, as if a slow-motion earthquake is constantly reinventing the surface.

When I arrive, tired after hiking up the last long incline alone, it is early afternoon, but very few people are around. I wander from tent to tent, looking at faces from many countries, but I can't find Henry Todd's camp. Finding my way over half the world to get here, I'm suddenly lost, not knowing how to find my team.

APRIL 18, 1996

We're just sitting around doing typical Base Camp stuff: talking, playing cards, reading, doing very little. That's what you have to do, I learned last year, to acclimatize. You have to drink water, baby yourself. I found the camp, and Jake had already begun fixing a place for our tent, leveling a platform of rocks. It took us all day yesterday to make a good home. And then, all night, I could hear cracks and moans of ice breaking and the water roaring beneath me like a waterfall.

All this downtime gives me a chance to check out the people around me, which I've been doing for three years now. One guy I meet, Göran Kropp, biked from Sweden to Everest with his mountain equipment. He intends to summit solo, and if he fails, he'll take his punishment—a plane home rather than a return bike trip. Another solo climber Jake and I met on the trail up here was a fashion plate of climber clothes, had a string of Sherpas, and spoke to no one. And then I finally met Michael, the missing member of our team, who arrived last night. Michael is in the Danish military, summited last year on the north side, and will videotape his climbing for his sponsor, Danish public TV.

Later, I sit in Scott Fischer's tent and Anatoli Boukreev comes in, wearing a Walkman and a big grin. He takes the tape out of his Walkman and soon has Russian folk songs blasting from Scott's tape deck. "You sing these Russian songs, you climb like me," he tells me as we listen to screeching voices.

He sits there, his gold teeth shining as he grins, and pulls out a piece of salami. Gnawing at it, he points it at me and offers more advice. "Eat this stuff, you summit easy." Eat that stuff and I'd be back in Kathmandu, sick in bed. It's called speck—almost pure animal lard, probably what makes the Russians such good climbers.

"Guess I'll never climb like you, then," I answer. "Couldn't do either one."

Scott just laughs at Anatoli. Two of the biggest names in climbing, and, sitting here, they treat me as an equal. That's true of most mountain people—none of this treating you like a rookie. They know you're in the same situation as they are.

everest '96

On the south side, we have to walk two weeks to get to Base Camp, but Camp One is only a half-day hike from Base Camp. We just have the little matter of the Khumbu Icefall to deal with. Take a platter of lumpy mashed potatoes with globs sticking up here and there—then let it dry out so you have overhanging stuff, uneven clumps, sharp edges, deep little cuts. Now, magnify that over a two-mile area, draw it up to 2,500 feet, and freeze it. But let some sections break off and others open up like little earthquakes at any time of the day or night, and you have some idea of the Khumbu Icefall. To summit Everest from the south—to get to Camp One, for that matter—every climber has to negotiate the Khumbu Icefall, a dangerous, 2,000-foot barrier.

Over sixty people have died in the Icefall. It's easy to see why. A section of ice could break off and hit you on the head. A crevasse could open up right under your feet. You could slip on one of the hundred ladders you cross. And the Icefall's always moving. Melting. Changing. So you never know. That's why they call crossing it roulette climbing. Like Russian roulette, you have only a one-in-six chance of getting the bullet rather than the empty chamber, but you never know. Especially if you play Russian roulette every day. That's what it's like, because you have to cross it every time you go up from Base Camp.

Henry brings us only about a third of the way in, and it seems pretty easy. The ice is sculptured into beautiful patterns, the sun is warm, and it's fun to be actually moving toward Everest. I quickly see the conditioning of members of our team. Some, like Thomas and Tina, poke along at a leisurely yak pace and then rest—frequently. Others, like Michael, Paul, Neil, and Graham, are in great condition, go hard, then rest: the speedy cockroach pace that so many Sherpas seem to use. I find my own pace—an easy, steady pace for about an hour, then rest to catch my breath.

Not much room to go very far or fast in the Icefall because of the ladders. Metal ladders are used to bridge crevasses, to negotiate sheer walls, to make getting to Camp One less of an obstacle course. These ladders are not, however, easy to cross, as I soon find out.

Picture a standard aluminum house ladder you'd use at home. Stretch it across a crevasse that is, say, an 8-foot-wide, 70-foot-deep split in the ice. Put crampons on your feet so that the only contact your feet have with the iced-over skinny rungs of the ladder, which has grown twisted and warped from glacier movement and use, is the little points on your crampons. Now wrap the loose rope on either side of the ladder around your arms and through your hands, lean forward so the ropes are tight, and let the rope slide through your hands as you cross the bouncy, clanging ladder. Careful how you place your feet so you don't let your crampons get caught on the rungs. And, just for fun, put a thirty-five-pound pack on your back, cold wind gusts in your face, and five people waiting for you to get across. If you want to get through the Icefall, you have maybe seventy ladders awaiting you, each its own adventure.

We get through our first encounter with the Icefall, each of us crossing our first ladders with Henry's advice. Because my foot is big enough to reach two rungs at a time, I can maintain my balance and get across fairly easily. For me, it's fun. Others with smaller feet, like Ray, have to be very careful on each rung.

APRIL 20, 1996

On my first trip to Camp One, I see firsthand how we play the odds every time up, thanks to my introduction to the Mousetrap, a particularly dangerous section of snow in the Icefall. Henry, Paul, Neil, Brigeete, and I make our way up a small hill, cross two ladders, then traverse sideways along a narrow ledge. Just above our heads, on this narrow ledge, is an overhang of snow jutting out like a roof over us. One look at the angle of the overhanging snow roof, large enough to snuff all five of us in a flash, shows me what roulette climbing is all about. The huge wedge of snow could go at any time—a slight shift in the glacier, a strong wind, or maybe even a sneeze, for all I know—and we'd be buried, trapped like mice. We scramble through the Mousetrap as quickly as we can, ten minutes at most, and struggle to the next ladder, glad for our small triumph.

Once out of the Icefall, we climb up to Camp One on a day of brilliant, warm sunshine. I follow Brigeete's good pace and get very warm, push sleeves up, and my arms are sunburned very quickly. On we go, using the fixed ropes up the steep slope, taking twenty steps, resting; twenty more, resting; rising far above the Icefall.

Soon I run into David Breashears, the filmmaker in charge of the IMAX expedition, coming down from Camp One. "Better get on that video journal," he says, and smiles. The New York producer had already spoken to him about what I was doing for National Geographic, and I guess he just wanted me to know he approved, or at least was not against what I was doing. He's making the official Everest documentary for IMAX, which will later exhibit the film on giant screens in special theaters and science museums. I'm no competition for his huge budget and crew, which is filming with wide-lens cameras for the big screen. And I'd just as soon do my camera work as quietly as possible, taking some footage here and there and keeping my camera out of sight. The main thing is to keep away from liaison officers, Nepali army officials assigned to keep an eye on everything we do. Breashears has an expensive official permit to film, but if his liaison officer happened to see me filming, I could be in for a lot of trouble. Jeff always told me not to risk trouble, but I know he wants as much footage as I can get. It's good to know David Breashears will not make it more difficult for me.

At Camp One, we help Jabion and the other Sherpas set up the tents, and soon we're inside. "We forgot drinks," Henry announces.

"I'll go down, be back before dark," I volunteer. It's a six-hour round trip that could completely waste me, but I'm ready for anything.

Henry looks shocked. "No! You can't do that! Save your energy. I'll come back up tomorrow." And he leaves.

I go outside and sit alone in the sun, looking off to the Icefall below us and the windswept summit of Everest high above, spreading my socks on my legs to dry, and quietly listen to Brigeete, Neil, and Paul, inside the tent, talk about their first sexual experiences. A very interesting way to spend an afternoon.

We sleep at Camp One to acclimatize. All night I hear the glacier moan and crack, a muffled sound of a huge tree snapping in half. And all night I'm bothered by headaches. In altitude, I'm learning that you just have to get used to having them, to try to lie as still as possible, to let it pound, and to drink lots of water for dehydration. But water, believe it or not, becomes a problem up here. I carry two quarts or so to drink on the way and, just as important, two cans of fuel to melt snow as soon as I get into the tent, but there's no way of preserving water: it freezes very quickly. So the only way to have a water supply is to light a stove and melt snow. Of course, there's plenty of snow around, but the process, from getting the stove set up to melting enough snow for drinking water, takes almost two hours—not what you want in the middle of a minus-20-degree night. I choose the headache instead—which I know is the wrong choice, but everybody does it.

APRIL 21, 1996

When I get back from Camp One, Jake is still at Base Camp, itchy to climb. He's been begging Henry to let him go up into the Icefall, pleads with Scott Fischer to climb with his team. But he has no permit to go beyond Base Camp. And so, I can't help myself, I rub it in just a little bit. I tell him how scary coming down through the Icefall is; how wobbly all the ladders seem; how, from up there, Base Camp looks like a miniature circus of color in the distant bleak gray and white of the glacier; how dehydrated and tired I am, just sitting there taking off my boots and stretching my legs and feeling him staring at me, so jealous of what I'm doing he can't sit still, frustrated because he can only watch.

We're in Base Camp for four days, and I know almost exactly what I'm going to do: eat as much as I can, drink plenty of water, and rest. Want to lose twenty-five pounds in a month? Then have *tsampa* (glue-thick barley flour mixed with milk tea) for breakfast, Sherpa stew (yak meat and curry) for dinner, tea (biscuits and cookies) at four o'clock, and leftovers for lunch at noon. In between, eat all the junk food you want, and you'll still lose weight. All you need to do is come here and climb every day. Guaranteed. You use 4,000 to 5,000 calories a day. You can't eat enough *tsampa* or Sherpa stew to keep up. So you lose twenty-five pounds. In my case, that's getting into muscle, because I have little body fat to begin with. That's why I sit around, play Perudo, an ancient Peruvian card game I bought at a Kmart back home, meet and talk to people from all over the world.

There are over five hundred people at Base Camp—more than a hundred climbers, plus Sherpas, Base Camp staff and support, plus liaison officers for each team so we don't violate some hidden rules. In addition, every team has a number of visitors dropping in to visit. But we have no loud music at night. Never happen, not even with Jake. The serious, high-altitude climbers are a small group of people, and we see each other frequently enough that we all become friends, or at least acquaintances. Almost everyone speaks English, and it's always very difficult to tell where anyone is from, although the Europeans always wear bright, fluorescent blues, pinks, and greens, and the Russians have terribly outdated equipment, and the Asians stay to themselves. But we're all unified by the desire to summit Everest and, therefore, respect each other enough that we don't need rules in camp. At least not many.

Our team did have a rule about swearing. Anyone caught swearing in Base Camp had to eat a mouthful of Marmite, an awful-tasting, mystery vegetable substance so thick it would gag a hog. Of course, I only heard about how it tasted; I never had any myself. Well, only a few times. If I brought that rule and Marmite home to my school, I know a lot of guys who'd be shoveling down Marmite all day.

One day some equipment was missing. Even though most people suspected visitors, the team leaders met to establish tough rules about stealing: any climber caught—off the trip; any Sherpa caught—out of a job; any leader caught—never back to Everest again. Tough rules, but you have to be able to leave your equipment around and not worry about someone stealing it.

APRIL 22, 1996

On the way to Camp Two, I'm so mad I could spit—if I had the energy. From Camp One, it's only about 1,000 feet higher to Camp Two, and less than two miles—which I run in about fifteen minutes at home—and already it's almost four hours because we have to take so many breaks. The sun's so hot I'm eating snow because my water's gone, even putting snow in my hat to cool off. And to make matters worse, potential crevasses force us to climb near the Lhotse-Nuptse Wall, where we can hear loosened rocks raining down too close for comfort.

All because of a stupid argument that kept us at Camp One until after ten o'clock, which got us out into the hottest part of the day. Hot. In the snow, on a glacier, on Mount Everest at almost 21,000 feet. Very hot. Direct sun off nothing but snow, heart pounding just taking a few steps with backpack, shirt soaked with sweat, no breeze, little water. Hot.

What I said before about Everest unifying us and how cooperative everyone is certainly did not apply to our team—not this morning. Henry radioed to us from Base Camp about plans for the day. (Two-way radios are the normal way to communicate on the mountain. There's even an emergency channel all expeditions tune to for emergencies.) It had snowed on our way to Camp One and all night, so he talked to Paul about conditions. As we were eating breakfast, packing to go to Camp Two, Paul and Michael, both experienced climbers, both veterans of Henry's trips, quietly discussed Henry's call by themselves. Thomas (and his other half, Tina), who had just about made it to Camp One before dark yesterday, immediately got in an uproar. "Don't hide conversations from the group!"

Well, that started it. Soon they were all yelling at one another.

"OK! Henry wants us to take some pots and stoves to Camp Two. Got that, Thomas?"

"I will not carry pots!"

"I didn't pay $24,000 to carry pots!"

I got into it. "Same as we all paid. You want high budget, go over to Rob Hall and pay $65,000!"

"If Henry says so, you will so carry those pots!"

Meantime the sun's getting higher, and these people are outside the tent without sunglasses, risking blindness just so they can argue. After I reminded them to put on their sunglasses, they came back for more.

"You think you can plan better, Thomas?" someone shouted. And they started all over again. Worse than ninth-grade kids.

Finally, we all just left in small groups. Michael and I just wanted out of earshot. Neil, Brigeete, and Paul walked off their fury. Thomas and Tina stayed behind to sulk. The whole thing reminded me of last year's Everest expedition. Adults.

They're the reason I'm struggling up to Camp Two right now. I'm so steamed my adrenaline gears up my pace, and soon I catch up to Rob Hall's Adventure Consultants team. Rob is a leader who's known for his expedition's high fees (almost triple what it cost me) and his precise planning. Today is an example. His climbers are all roped up to one another for safety, and here I come, completely un-roped, so dehydrated in the hot sun I'm eating snow. We stop to rest and I meet Rob and Beck Weathers, a doctor from Texas; Andy Harris, a guide; and Yasuko Namba, a Japanese woman. While they're kidding me about getting out of school, about being sixteen on Everest, I wonder which one is Jon Krakauer, a writer who was supposed to come to Everest on our team last year. I smile and secretly envy them the water they're drinking; I'm that thirsty. I will not, however, ask for any water. It's my own fault for being unprepared. I can't expect climbers to give up the water they need to someone careless like me. I'll just have to eat snow and wait till I reach to Camp Two.

As we get closer to Camp Two, one of our Sherpas passes us on his way down and tells me to look for the big white tent, which I see amid all the colored tents off in the distance. Camp Two is really Advanced Base Camp, so there are many tents—must be a hundred and fifty, for all the support people and supplies. It's good to be able to spot our tent right away.

The more I think about the way adults behave, the more I wonder. Coming up to Camp One yesterday was a snowy, windy, slow hike. All I wanted was to get inside the tent, inside my warm sleeping bag. I had purposely left my sleeping bag there; we all use two so we don't have to keep carrying them up and down. When I got there, Henry was already inside the tent and inside my sleeping bag, warm as toast.

So yesterday we got into the same sort of stupid argument those other guys did this morning. "Henry, that's my sleeping bag!" I said. Of course, Henry said it was his—the bags look alike. "Yours must be in the other tent." It was late; it was cold; it had been a tough climb. All I have to sleep in is my down suit. I'm thinking, I'm gonna kill this guy. He's in my sleeping bag! I started yelling, just like Thomas. "Henry, I left it right where you are!" Henry looked around, said slowly, "All right. Someone must have stolen it. I'll go back down." And he left.

Score one for me, I guess. But I keep thinking, as I get to the long uphill to Camp Two, that it's so foolish to argue over little things. We have to depend on each other for our lives up here, and we get into the little kid stuff I thought I had left back in junior high—last year.

I straggle behind Rob's team, and, when I finally pass his dining tent, he invites me in for tea. Rob introduces me to Jon Krakauer, and the three of us sit at a table drinking delicious, warm, thirst-quenching tea, talking about Rob's previous trips to Everest.

We talk for a while about the '95 expedition Jon missed. Soon Michael comes by, and we set off for our camp.

When we finally get to the big white tent, it looks left in a hurry, with pots on the stove, lots of equipment, even packages of chocolate cookies. After one look around, I know that it isn't ours, that ours is not up yet, that it may be Mal Duff's. Mal is, like Henry, a Scottish climber and expedition leader, and a good friend of Henry's. Although we know it isn't our tent, we stay anyway. We even sample some chocolate cookies (just one small package). Paul, Neil, and Brigeete come in, still fuming, but Thomas and Tina never show. Just as well.

APRIL 23, 1996

As we are about to leave in the morning, who should arrive but Mal Duff's team, wondering who we are. We try to explain our "big white tent" mistake. They look a little annoyed, but at least Mal doesn't fine us the $100 that is standard for using someone else's tent. Michael and I don't say a word about the cookies, and we just kind of slink off down the mountain.

APRIL 25, 1996

Third time through the Icefall. Back up to Camp One. Michael and I have our video cameras and are filming. We switch cameras to get each other climbing. We climb up a bit, then stop to do a few takes of each other across a difficult ladder or to get good angles in a crevasse. Henry's yelling at us to get through the Icefall—fast—but we want to get some good footage and we do retakes of each other. It's really fun to film today, to notice the changes in the Icefall, to climb past house-size blocks of ice that were not there last time up. Then up the short, steep killer hill to Camp One.

We rest at Camp One, hoping for cloud cover to make climbing to Camp Two easier. In fact, the climbing is generally easier for me now. I'm not nearly as tired reaching Camp One and have plenty left to get to Camp Two, all in one day. Even going down to Base Camp yesterday was easier. Acclimatizing works!

I have to be honest, though, and say that while I have enough energy to get to Camp Two, my legs are kind of dead, not really strong. Once you start the process of these repeated climbs up and down the mountain, carrying a heavy pack, you never get your legs back. But you do develop an automatic energy-saver that kicks into gear anytime. Instead of stepping up on rock and pulling all your weight up with your quads, you look for a way around it. Same is true coming down. You try to relax your leg muscles as much as possible between steps. After a while it becomes part of your walking style, to be efficient in every movement, to keep some energy in the tank. Say some guy 500 feet above you breaks a leg. If you're wasted, you can't be of much help. In Base Camp there are no volleyball nets, only card games.

All that conditioning back home really pays off for me here, but I'm finding out I'm an exception. Al Burgess may run up mountains to train, and Roger Gocking runs distance races; Neal Beidleman, an aerospace engineer from Colorado, runs 75- and 100-mile races. But most high-altitude climbers are not in great shape. Henry has a big ol' butt, and trains by doing a little bike riding. Thomas and Tina did karate to train. Even Reinhold Messner, who has climbed all fourteen 8,000-meter peaks without oxygen, was tested and found to have quite an ordinary lung capacity. His only difference was mental. And that's what all the high-altitude climbers have in common: the mental capacity to push themselves to take the next step, and to know that they can keep taking that next step, no matter what. You have to know that you can push far beyond what you thought was your limit.

Michael and I are climbing and filming our way to Camp Two. I look back and see Henry climbing with Scott Fischer below us—two black dots on the brilliant white snow.

From behind them, I can see a fog moving up the Western Cwm. (*Cwm* is a Welsh term for "valley" or "cirque.") The sun hits the fog in just the right way to give it an orange-brown glow, making it seem like a huge solid blanket rolling silently toward me. One second Henry and Scott are in sunshine—then, poof! Gone, eaten up by the blanket. Another second, and poof! I'm covered, too. I can see only a few feet in front on me, can only follow the ropes and the bamboo wands stuck in the snow to define the route in bad weather. It's OK, though. Camp Two will be easy to find, even in the fog. I shouldn't call it fog. Fog intrudes on our space. *Clouds* is more accurate. We climbers intrude on their clouds!

APRIL 26, 1996

At Base Camp you see trekkers, visitors, and support people; the only people you see up here at Camp Two are part of an exclusive club, stopping off at 21,000 feet on the way up. Camp Two can accommodate almost two hundred people, but is only about half filled most of the time—literally a climber's "upper class." But the food's far from exclusive—chicken supreme over rice just about every meal—and the sleeping arrangements are worse. Take Henry and Michael and all our equipment in one small tent, then try to sleep in the middle. Especially with Henry growling at me to be still when I have no pillow. How can they possibly expect me to sleep with wadded-up clothes rather than a down pillow?

At least the headaches are not as bad, and I'm doing OK until

Henry gets on my case about getting dressed faster. Here's a guy whose fastest pace is yak pace, and he's telling me to move. He's always on my case, it seems, watching over me, because if anything were to happen to me, he'd probably be called a child abuser.

APRIL 27, 1996

Strange as it may seem, there are always people on Everest, going from one camp to another, acclimatizing. (Even members of teams get separated by their schedules. For example, I don't see much of Ray Dorr because we happen to be on different acclimatizing schedules.) All of us climb over 70 percent of Everest a number of times, just to be ready for that one shot at the top. As a result, one of the biggest problems climbing to Camp Three, at almost 25,000 feet, is traffic. Think of going up a steep, narrow country path, wide enough for one person but a path that everyone must use in both directions, and you get a sense of the traffic jam. The path in our case is the fixed rope to Camp Three. Because it's so steep, windy, and cold at that altitude, you always clip onto the rope. Everyone does. Thus the traffic jam.

When you meet someone coming down or are passing someone going up, there's a little dance you have to do. You unclip from the rope, dangerous at that steep an angle, grab hold of the other guy's clothes, edge around him as he hangs on to the rope with both hands, then clip on again. Do this dance four or five times as I do, and you can't help but think it's a traffic jam at 24,000 feet.

Graham Ratcliffe and I are the first two members of our team to go to Camp Three. We spent time together on Everest '95, where he was on Henry's team. He's in his forties, a good climber—he summited—and a good guy to talk to. Graham and I really want to summit together this year.

Of course, we all want to summit together, but realistically we know it won't happen. Even within our group, there are different levels of ability, of strength. Neil, Paul, Michael, and Brigeete are all strong, capable climbers, but Henry has designated Graham and me to be the first of the team to go to the summit. Does Henry have my record in mind? Not at all. And neither do I, nor anyone else. I'm just here to climb now. Henry knows Graham and I are ready and able, and he's had to plan how he wants his team to operate.

So he gave Graham and me the go-ahead for Camp Three.

If we're going to get into the best position to summit, we have to go to Camp Three, then go down to about 13,000 feet to rest for three days. (Base Camp, at 17,000 feet, is too high to get the rest you need.) Then you go all the way back up to Camp Four, a day ahead of summit attempt. The others will follow at one-day intervals. All very carefully planned.

The only drawback to going down to 13,000 feet is the potential for sickness. Let's face it: this is the third world, where so much is dirt and where you come in contact with so many sick people, trekkers, Nepali, and Sherpas in the teahouses along the route that inevitably you're going to get sick.

At this altitude, my progress is very good—if I can hold my pace at five sets of twenty steps, then a rest stop, gasping for breath in the thin air. Five more sets of twenty steps and rest again. Plenty of time to think on the way to Camp Three. I think about the cold wind and snow, and the little steps I'm taking to get up the highest mountain in the world at exactly 10:14 A.M., and picture the people walking along at this very same moment in shorts and shirts in the little green villages far below us, and the empty seat in the history class I'd be in right now back home. I look up at Everest, whose summit is almost 5,000 feet higher than where I am now, and I think how far I have to go. Then I cut myself off from that thought and get back to the reality of getting to Camp Three. That's my goal today. Camp

Three. One step at a time. Or twenty steps at a time. The only way to go.

When the climbing gets hard, I think that by tomorrow none of this discomfort or pain will make any difference. Same as when I'm home, and I might as well get the most out of a run—go the long way, add another two miles, the next twenty minutes will go by anyway, might as well get the most out of it. Then I think, all the minutes of my life go by the same way. Whether I work hard at something or play around, whether I eventually become a doctor, or lawyer, or work for waste management—the time will still pass by and I'll either be using the time well, intensely, or just waiting for something to happen.

Good to remind myself of that, especially when up ahead near Camp Three, Babu, one of the Sherpas, and Tierry, a Frenchman with the South African team, are throwing stuff out of their campsite. Typical Everest camp: climbers and Sherpas leave their garbage all over the place. Fuel canisters and small plastic containers come whizzing by my head. "Hey, Babu, wanna knock that off before you kill me?" I yell into the wind. Babu turns, surprised to see me, and smiles that big, friendly Sherpa smile.

The comfort of camps on Everest gets reduced the higher you go. The circus city of Base Camp is reduced to the solid no-nonsense of Camp One. The primitive but adequate sharing of Camp Two is reduced to wherever you can get a tent up on the steep face of Camp Three, a campsite no one would ever pick. Yeah, the view's terrific, but try to hack a notch into the side of such a steep slope of ice and put tents there. We have no other choice, so we help Jabion and the other Sherpas dig out a platform in the snow and set up our tent. We can only dig into the ice so far, after all. And what we're doing is outrageously strenuous at 24,000 feet, which means that a corner of the tent and floor jut out from the side of the slope, like a house on the side of an ocean cliff, and all you can put on that end of the tent is your feet. The mountain face is scary steep here, so much so that when you come out of the tent you must immediately grab onto a rope.

I heard about one guy who came out of his tent up here, half asleep, forgot the rope and slid off the mountain. I don't play around. I make sure the poles are tight, get into the tent into my sleeping bag, cook some ramen noodles, ignore the headache, and try to sleep, hoping the night will pass quickly at this, the highest point I've ever slept.

the storm

MAY 2, 1996

Middle of the night. A teahouse in Gorak Shep. I chew vitamins and herb supplements, trying to sleep. I keep thinking about the operation my mom told me about. My father has had ear infections for years. Finally, last week he went to a doctor, who's going to do a small operation, clean out the infection, and reconstruct his eardrum. It'll be good for him to get rid of the ear infections once and for all.

Graham and I met my mom and her friend Carrie today on the trail down to Dingboche, where Graham and I had gone to rest. After going to Camp Three three days ago, we knew we needed a change. We brought up extra equipment for our summit attempt: overboots, oxygen masks, extra glove liners, batteries for boot heaters. Then we headed back down to Base Camp. What took two days to climb up we descended in six hours—including a stop at Camp One and passing the always adventurous Icefall. Breathing was easier, of course, but the long descent was so jarring on the legs that to sit finally in Base Camp and taste the cold Tang was just what I needed. I couldn't eat, though. Pasang made a good meal, and I needed to replace all those calories. But I just couldn't do it. No appetite at all. The Everest Crash Diet strikes again. By now my stomach has shrunk; I'm losing weight, losing strength, and all I want is sleep.

My mother liked Nepal so much when she came to Ama Dablam last year that she wanted to come to Base Camp, along with Carrie, for the final ten days of our trip. I knew she was hiking somewhere along the trail, scheduled to be here soon, but it was strange to be walking around a curve on a dirt trail in the mountains of Nepal and then practically knock down a little lady who turned out to be my mother! After we talked for a while, I had a difficult decision to make. Should I go down lower, get more rest (and possibly expose myself to sickness) or, after spending the night here in Gorak Shep, go back to Base Camp with my mom, have time with her and rest less, but stay in a better environment? Base Camp won. You can't rest in these teahouses, anyway.

In the bunks below me are eleven trekkers from India. All of them are coughing; one is chanting. In the bunks next to me are my mother and Carrie. The air is alive with coughing, chanting. No one sleeps. I wonder if my mom likes Nepal now.

MAY 4, 1996

Base Camp. By now Michael, Brigeete, Paul, and Neil have all gone to Camp Three and are resting, almost ready to go. It took Thomas and Tina eight hours to get through a forty-five-minute section of the Icefall; they're better off in Base Camp, where Henry and Ray are resting.

We decide on May 8 as summit day. Timing has to be perfect. You need a calm, clear advance forecast, preferably with a full moon for a three A.M. start. You also need to have everyone healthy and at Camp Two days ahead of summit day. May 8 fills the bill!

Or at least May 8 seems right until Göran Kropp gets involved. He's the solo climber who biked from Sweden, and he wants to ride home after he summits. He's the first climber up this season, and naturally everyone wants to know what conditions are like up near the peak. As we get ready, we're constantly in touch with Kropp's girlfriend, who reports that he's turning around because of waist-deep powder snow.

Deep powder might be great for skiers, but for climbers at 28,000 feet it's sheer torture. Imagine walking through snow so fine that each footstep instantly fills in, so it's always an unbroken trail. Imagine the snow up to your waist and feel it just holding you down. Now take that up to 28,000 feet, and the sheer effort of moving ten, twenty feet becomes overwhelming. You work your butt off to get nowhere. Certainly not to the top of Everest.

The news spreads. Scott Fischer and Rob Hall come by with a plan. They're going to aim for May 10 and ask other teams not to go up that day. Their teams are large, and no one wants to be on a crowded mountain. Most teams agree that a crowded mountain is a dangerous mountain. If we want to go before, in our case the eighth, our target date, fine. Yet if we do go on the eighth, we have guaranteed good conditions but only a few climbers to break trail through the powder. If we go on the eleventh, we have thirty to fifty climbers and Sherpas breaking trail the day before. A difficult decision, believe it or not. Here's why: Warm air pushes the jet stream up into the atmosphere for a short time, giving Everest a "summer" of three to ten days of manageable climate. After the tenth of May or so, the jet stream usually starts to drop back down to its normal storm-producing position. Last year on the north side, Everest was storm-free long enough to allow eighty-eight climbers to summit. Considering only sixty-six had ever summited on the north side before that, you can see the weather's impact. Particularly when only one person summited here on the south side the whole season, where storms just kept coming.

Taking a chance on the possibility of changing conditions makes more sense to Henry than trying to climb above Camp Four in deep powder that squeezes the energy right out of you. Better to let all those climbers pack down the snow. The rest of us agree. May 11 it is.

MAY 8, 1996

Through the Icefall to Camp One, then to Camp Two. A clear, beautiful day. So calm the mountain is silent, so clear and warm it's driving me crazy. A perfect day to summit. Wasted.

But it feels so good to be moving. I've been at Base Camp since May 4, which is too much time to sit around. If my mom and Carrie weren't there to talk to, I know I'd spend too much time sorting through my stuff, repacking, double-checking, listening to music, getting anxious. I don't think I'm going to fall. And I certainly don't think I'm going to die. I have confidence in my climbing skills. You have to. Otherwise forget it. You can't fake it.

I get anxious because I've been too healthy; should have gotten sick earlier in the trip, gotten it out of my system. I have a cold now, and it's getting worse by the hour—a persistent cough, with a lot of phlegm, not like last year's cough, which was a dry hack. But I'm strong after all that sitting in Base Camp. Camp Two is a tiring, but manageable, one-day trip. After our break at Camp One, I look up to the summit and realize that just at this moment, around one o'clock today, May 8, Graham and I had planned to be there, looking down at the very slope I'm climbing.

The whole crew gets to Camp Two in good shape. Even Thomas and Tina make it, a few hours late but give them credit, they're still with us.

MAY 9, 1996

On the way to Camp Three, I get some good video of the steep Lhotse Face. The camera is a definite burden, but I'm still trying to get some of the shots the crew wants.

A rescue team brings an injured climber down past Jabion and me. His only mistakes were to climb out of his tent at Camp Three unroped and to forget how steep the terrain was, which is easy to do when your brain's not working very well due to lack of oxygen and fatigue. He slid hundreds of feet down the angled ice. He's not expected to live.

MAY 10, 1996

Jabion and I are working our way from Camp Three up the Geneva Spur and across the yellow band of rock to Camp Four, when we are suddenly belted with an unexpected force of wind and snow. What was up to now difficult and uncomfortable now takes on a new component: danger. Every step now becomes a triumph, every minute to Camp Four increasingly painful. In the late afternoon, the wind howls through a snowstorm so intense, the snow feels like a solid wall. We manage to stumble toward the faint yellow glow of the lights coming from the tents at Camp Four. Jabion and I have not spoken or taken off our masks for at least an hour. If we could talk, I'd tell him how glad I am to be so near the safety of those tents. I turn away from the tents for a moment and imagine how it would feel to have only the gathering dark and snow to look at, and what courage it would take to face that empty, screeching, black night.

Later, I'm half asleep when I feel like gagging. Jabion has put my oxygen mask over my face, trying to help me get through the night. Up to now, I've been breathing fairly well. Once I get over 21,000 feet, I seem to adjust and don't struggle as much as most climbers. But now I appreciate Jabion for keeping an eye on me, because suddenly I've been coughing my mountain hack, big time, feeling weaker and weaker, and the inevitable hits me. We will not summit. Not tomorrow.

I can no longer even doze, with the wind screaming and snapping the edges of the tent, packed as I am into a jumble of sleeping bags of Sherpas. I start to think about how these Sherpas work in these storms all the time. The Sherpas climb the same difficult terrain as we do, but somehow for them it's easier. Often they don't use oxygen. One older Sherpa I know, Ang Rita, has summited Everest nine times. Without oxygen. Maybe they're just a superior race.

One day on the trek up to Base Camp, I stopped in a village where I saw a guy about Jabion's size—five feet six or so—walking along carrying a load of rolled-up tin. Tin is important for housing in Nepal, and so you see guys carrying it around. This tin looked like a giant roll of paper towels, about seven feet high and two feet thick, balanced on his neck and shoulders by a head strap. When he put the tin down to rest, I went over to it to see how far I could carry it. I tried to pick it up—couldn't move it! I looked around to see if anyone was watching—no one was—and tried again. Nope. Still couldn't budge it. Here I was, a good six or seven inches taller, and maybe fifty pounds more of hard-worked muscle, yet that little porter came over, rigged his head strap, and walked away with the tin as if it really were a giant roll of paper towels! He did have, I must admit, incredibly strong legs, as if his lower half belonged to an NFL linebacker. But strong legs or not, I was amazed to see him go off up the trail, bent over by the weight of the tin.

I requested Jabion to go on this trip, and he knows how difficult that is to pull off. Every Sherpa wants Everest on his résumé, a great credential to have, like a college degree in the United States. With it, you get good jobs; without it, you're always minor league. That's

why I requested Jabion—he had never been to Everest. The agency
he works for wasn't working this trip at all. So I had to see Kami, our
sirdar, or Sherpa boss, and request Jabion, which meant one of
Kami's regular guys couldn't work. The problem is Kami usually
hires relatives—most Sherpas do—and that put Jabion in an awkward place. He has to work with those people much more than with
me. But it all worked out well, because Jabion proved to be one of
the strongest Sherpas and got along well with everyone—climbers
and Sherpas alike.

MAY 11, 1996

Pasang looks out of the tent, sees a star above the South Col, and
immediately shoves his stuff into his rucksack and is gone into the
thundering wind. Jabion says, "Bad luck to see a star that bright in
morning." He may be right. Paul had already gone down from Camp
Three. Jabion, Graham, and I decide to go down, too. I still don't
know about Ray, who was missing last night. Brigeete, Neil, and
Michael plan to wait out the wind and summit tomorrow. Fat chance
they'll have to summit.

I get out of the tent, feeling very spaced out and weak after
coughing all night, struggle to get crampons on, struggle to get backpack, oxygen mask on. Have to rest after each effort. Shocked to see
Pete Athans, one of the best climbers, coming up. How did he get
here so early? "Rob Hall's still up there," he says. I look up and see,
in the early light, a string of black dots working up the slope. A rescue team. "At least nine people missing. Don't know for sure." He
radios to Base Camp that I'm coming down and takes off for the rescue mission. Pete's amazingly strong to go up in that storm. I stand
watching him for a moment. Nine people? Who? I look up the mountain, imagine trying to grope through a whiteout with dark coming
on, imagine trying to find our tents, the smallest possible needle in

the huge haystack of Everest, especially when your brain can hardly function, and I realize how lucky I was to be in a tent.

Jabion and I go back over the Geneva Spur, fighting the wind for balance on each rocky step. How strong that wind is, trying to pluck us off the mountain with one gust, trying to flatten us with the next. And then, once across, we round a corner and are suddenly wind free, protected by the spur we just traversed. Soon the sun comes out, we warm up, and, as we descend, off come the mask, the heavy mittens, the heavy coat.

Haven't had much solid food now for four days. Can't seem to force anything down. Lack of appetite and coughing have weakened me to the point that I can only take about ten steps before I have to rest. Jabion stays with me, and it is very slow going. In fact, a group of climbers from Scott Fischer's team passes me. They look awful, in much worse shape than I am. They tell me they had been caught by the storm, were lucky to make it back to camp. And then one guy tells me Scott is dead. One of the best in the world, a climber who's survived some terrible situations, has died. They don't know exactly what happened. He seemed OK, then they lost sight of him. They leave for Camp Three, some of them frostbitten, all exhausted and devastated by Scott's death. I take ten more steps before resting again.

When Jabion and I get to Camp Three, Fischer's team have already set their backpacks into the steep slope and are sitting on them in the sun. They just lost their great friend and leader, are lucky to be alive themselves, and they just sit there, numb. Neal Beidleman mumbles something about Scott's dying being his fault; the others get on his case, deny there was anything he could have done. I sit with them. The scary pitch of the slope here at Camp Three seems safe now compared to the howling nightmare of Camp Four, but I don't know what to say.

Scott had been friendly to me, invited me over to his tent, helped me with my camera, and now he's dead—same trip, same mountain, not far from me. And I can't think about it now. Everything is so confusing. All the order and scheduling gone, all the acclimatizing, oxygen masks, foot warmers—none of it seems to matter now. It is just the fate of survival as to who makes it. I'm in a tent and make it. Some of them make it back to their tents; others don't. I'm the first climber these tired, beaten people have seen. I should say something consoling but I can't. No way to analyze or talk. Just sit in the sun for a moment, then head down to Base Camp.

My dad was a police officer for years, but he wasn't the one to go to the parents' house at two A.M. to tell them about their kids' accidents. His partner, Jack, did that. Same for me. I just can't talk right now. Neither can they. We all just sit there a while, hacking. We're all gaunt, sunburned, dirty, with constant coughs.

I load up all my equipment: sleeping bag, clothes, oxygen tank, accessories, and the video camera, and start to leave Camp Three. I never even used the video camera up there. National Geographic Special? Forget it. It was enough just to survive. I know there was a lot of time and money invested, and I was expected to get my share of filming done. But right now, I really can't care. I could never film Scott Fischer's people at Camp Three. No way I'm doing that. I'm not intruding on them.

I tell Jabion to go ahead. I'll go down myself. Let momentum pull me.

Hold on to rope, slide down. Rest. I meet David Breashears going up for rescue. He congratulates me. My legs are cramping, my eyes hurt, the roof of my mouth is burned, I'm coughing, my back hurts from the heavy pack, and I'm so weak I can walk only ten steps before resting. Congratulations? He must think I summited. "I didn't summit," I mumble.

"So what," he says. "You're alive." And takes off. I watch him go and think: He's right. Don't feel sorry for yourself. You wanted to be here. Your pilgrimage. And you are still alive. So pay attention and get down the mountain!

That's what I do. I pay attention. Even though I'm really scared for the first time, with crevasses everywhere, alone, unroped, fatigued, I won't let Scott Fischer into my mind; I won't think about falling; I won't panic. I go fast. Have to get to Camp Two.

Into the kitchen tent. Hot orange drink. Someone tells me Ray's OK. He spent the whole awful night outside, lost his backpack with sleeping bag, down suit, glasses—just about everything—stumbled around, turned up at Camp Three. Ray's a tough New Yorker. Last year on our trip to the north side of Everest, he grabbed the wrong rope, fell forty feet, landed in snow, wandered around, fell into a crevasse, got out, and showed up later that night. I struggle to our tent, where I find Ray, along with Henry, Paul, and Graham, talking about the rumors, the reports of deaths, the missing climbers. Henry's furious with Brigeete, Neil, and Michael for staying at Camp Four and not becoming involved with the rescue. I send a message to my mom to let her know I'm OK, crawl into my sleeping bag, and go to sleep.

MAY 12, 1996

For a while everything seems normal, as if all those people hadn't died, as if no one was missing, as if the horrible night had never happened. Like the end of one of those horror movies when all the actors stand around wondering where they're going for coffee while the dead monster's thick body gets ignored. Maybe that's what people do when someone dies—maybe they still laugh and kid around. That's what seems to be happening here. We're ignoring death.

Halfway across a crevasse in the Icefall, my crampon gets stuck on a ladder. It's a wide, very deep crevasse, spanned by three ladders tied together. That's the problem. I wedge the back edge of my crampon into the overlap of two rungs. It won't budge. Kind of symbolic of this trip. Get stuck in Camp Four very near the summit, now stuck in the Icefall, with Base Camp within sight. My weak condition makes it worse, of course, but it's tricky enough. I'm on a swaying ladder. Kami, our lead Sherpa, who has caught up to me, cannot come out and free me, because the ladder might pull away from its anchor with the weight of the two of us and send us both down into a crevasse that seems to go all the way to Kathmandu.

Finally, I take the crampon off and just leave it there. When I get off the ladder, Kami tries to work it free. One little nudge from him and it goes flying down onto an ice ledge about twenty feet down, leaving me to slip and slide the rest of the way down.

Near Base Camp, Scott Fischer's team passes me, laughing at me about my crampon, which they saw in the crevasse. Charlotte Fox hugs me; a group of Sherpas swoop by, whooping and laughing in the soft snow. We're almost home. Neal Beidleman stops with me, offers a packet of Reload, and I can feel the carbohydrate gel give me energy. "Is it true you run ultramarathons?" I ask him.

"Yeah, I do. And you know what? They're easier than trying to climb Everest."

Once into Base Camp, reality roars back. My mother finds me, gives me a big hug, blurts out, "Thank God. You're alive!" She hadn't known if I was safe or not during the storm—she hadn't eaten or slept at all for two days. She and Carrie wandered from camp to camp, their hopes rising and falling with each rumor. Someone would tell her I was dead, then someone else would say I was alive. Elated after finally learning I was OK, she and Carrie were saddened again when they listened, as so many did in Base Camp, to Rob Hall speak his last words to his wife on the phone. Rob had stayed near the summit to help one of his clients, Doug Hansen. Both were far beyond the reach of any rescue. After Doug died, Rob lived long enough to radio down and ask to speak to his wife in New Zealand. Base Camp was able to get his call through, and everyone listened as Rob spoke his last words to his wife, pregnant with their first child.

Around Base Camp I see the usual unraveling, the normal sense of everything kind of used up that always happens at the end of a trip. This time everything gets magnified by the storm—by death. People leave; tents that are usually neat and well organized are by now a mess of wadded-up clothes. There is no music from Rob Hall's camp. And climbers, even the ones who an hour ago were coming down laughing, are now quiet, talking in whispers. Base Camp has lost its leaders, Rob Hall and Scott Fischer, and everyone feels their absence.

I want to respond to my mother's sense of relief, to her happiness, to her running around getting me hot drinks and food, but I can't. I have little to say. I'm far too numbed by fatigue and my cough to think of anything but sleep. No food. Just a little water and sleep.

MAY 13, 1996

Helicopter noise wakes Base Camp early. I stumble out and find out that Beck Weathers and Makalu Gau, the leader of the Taiwanese expedition, are still alive after two nights on the mountain and are being helicoptered out by a Nepali pilot courageous enough to attempt the highest helicopter flight ever, landing high above the Icefall. Then later, Charlotte Fox, Sandy Hill Pittman, and Tim Madsen are taken out of Base Camp by helicopter because of frostbite.

I call my dad to tell him I'm OK, that I'll rest up and try to summit again in a few days. I start to ask him about the ear operation and he interrupts. "Mark, just come home now. Okay?" Then a long pause. I think I can hear him crying on the other end. I never heard him or saw him cry before. "Get someone to get your stuff down from Camp Four and just come home." Another long pause. Must be crying. But why? Glad I made it through the storm? His operation?

"OK." I'm ready. I can do that. Funny. I don't argue for another attempt. I don't need convincing. As if my father's tone and words are exactly what I need, I want, suddenly, nothing more than to go home. Once you start thinking of home, that's all that matters. You're so sick, ugly, dirty, wasted, skinny, and sunburned that all you want now is your own bed, and that momentum pulls you home.

MAY 14, 1996

I am talking to Morton Dean of *Good Morning America*; we are live across the United States. He's asking me about surviving the storm, about the temperatures and winds, and what I know. ABC wants me because I am the youngest climber, but they should get someone who knows more. I tell him I'm not sure of the temperature; I was in a tent and didn't see most of the problems, and even now I'm not sure of the final death toll. I'm distracted during our phone call because I don't want to be here. I want to be at a memorial service for Scott Fischer, which is being held as I talk. The whole Base Camp is there for a great guy and climber, but because we had technical problems, my call was delayed, and now I'm on the phone saying stupid things like "Yeah. It was very cold and windy up there."

As I talk, I can picture Ray, Henry, Graham, and the rest of our crew standing in the afternoon sun, the wind blowing their hair, everyone battle weary—Sherpas, climbers, support people—all together in a scene out of a World War II movie. And I'm battle weary, too—in a tent reporting back to headquarters about this great battle that the enemy won, which left some scarred, some dead, all of us shaken.

Maybe it's appropriate that I get stuck with a media problem—the kid who gets all the publicity because he's so young and his parents must be irresponsible to let him climb the world's highest mountain. But I'm not one of the dead climbers, or even one of the frostbitten ones. And I know I'll be back next year. They say you always make it on the third try. Most people learn how to acclimate, to be patient, and they summit on the third try.

Next spring for me. The magic of the third try.

When I finish talking to *Good Morning America*, I realize that the phone I've been using in the New Zealand tent is the one used to get Rob Hall's final call to his wife just before he died. It's hard to think anything positive about Everest right now, a force that tricks people into tranquil sunshine, then smacks them with a killer wind. Enemy. That's all I can think of. An enemy I want to get away from.

MAY 18, 1996

Henry's still mad at Brigeete, Neil, and Michael about the rescue. You can tell. He's sitting there with his head in his hands and scowling at the floor.

"I'm telling you," Brigeete says. "Our radio was out. We knew nothing. The South African team would not lend us theirs. We knew nothing!"

Our team is in Base Camp. No one summited. Thomas and Tina barely made it to Camp Two. Ray's lucky to be alive. Michael, Neil, Brigeete, Paul, and I were forced down by the wind. Henry and Graham got sick. But we're all alive. And I'm out of here.

Carrie, my mother, Graham, and I reverse all the villages we saw on the way up. We descend to Thugla. Pangboche. All a blur. Too tired to carry my own backpack—my ribs hurt—I hire a porter.

Then to Syangboche for a helicopter out to Kathmandu. Next flight?
Three days. Two flights out per day. Twenty-four per flight. Too many
climbers, Sherpas, and trekkers coming down from the mountain.

MAY 20, 1996

Sit around. Stand around. Stare at each other. Rest. That's Syangboche. Then, last flight out, a guy comes running up. "One seat!"
Graham and I look at each other. "You," Graham says. I stuff
my bag, leave my mom and Carrie, and get to Kathmandu. With
no money! I had accidentally left all but a few rupees with my
mother.

While reporters attack climbers off the helicopter with questions
about the storm, I spend my only rupees on a cab to our hotel (they
know me—I can charge everything); take the longest, sweetest
shower, the first in two months; then eat: chicken, double order of
French fries, two pieces of chocolate cake, then more chicken.

I can't sleep. My ribs hurt, and my breathing becomes more
shallow, as if I'm running hospital stairs. I call the front desk for a
doctor. An hour later a weird-looking guy with hair coming out of his
nose comes in. He examines me. "You have slight pneumonia, left
lung. I give you injection." He takes a syringe and a thick needle
from a paper towel.

"What are you giving me?"

"Help you breathe."

I'm getting nervous. "Is that a clean needle?"

"You want a clean needle? I can get you clean needle."

"Of course a clean needle!" Do I let him do this?

He gives me the shot, promises to return with prescriptions and
vitamin C.

"You have money?"

I shake my head.

"But you have to pay!" He's looking at me, not believing what he's hearing. An American in a good hotel and no money?

Tomorrow, I tell him, my mother will come with the $70. He tells me he'll be here at noon and stomps out.

Codeine slows my body and mind, so when I call my father, I'm a bit fuzzy. When I say hello, he starts crying. Just like the other day. I want to ask about the operation, but he blurts out, "Mark, they got all the cancer out."

"Cancer? What cancer? It's an ear infection!"

"No, Mark. It's cancer. The infection became cancer. A twelve-hour operation, but they got it all."

I start to cry. Both of us sobbing into the phone, as far away from each other as it is possible to be and still be on the planet. Oh, God! Please, God! Cancer? Not this strong cop who dives down to submerged cars and saves young girls, who disarms would-be murderers with shotguns, who operates on three hours of sleep for years and years. Impossible.

"I couldn't tell you before. I wanted Mom and you here so bad. But I didn't want you thinking about me and getting distracted. It's too dangerous up there."

I can't talk. All I can do is cry. He tells me to have Mom call him. I mumble good-bye and crawl into bed. I try to sleep, but all I can think of is what it must be like inside his ear. I think about the stories I heard when I was a kid about those earwig bugs.

How if one got in your ear, it would eat and burrow its way into your head. I feel earwigs crawling all over my head, trying to get into my ear, and see earwigs scurrying all over the heads of the corpses of the climbers on Everest, and I wake up coughing and sweating and wanting to scream. But I am a little kid alone in a hotel room in Kathmandu, and my mother is in Syangboche and my father is far away in Rhode Island, and neither one will hear.

MAY 21, 1996

Pacing the hotel lobby waiting for my mom, figuring out what to say. Already paid the doctor, who showed up here promptly at twelve. Charlotte Fox lent it to me. Funny to walk into the Yak and Yeti Hotel and find a number of climbers sitting around the pool, enjoying their slow recovery from Everest. I come in scruffy, almost bent over from the pneumonia and my father's news.

My mother walks into the lobby. She must read the look on my face because when I say, "Got some news. . . ." she gets that steely look she gets. And when I say, "Dad has cancer in his ear," she bolts to her room to call him, and I go off to repay Charlotte.

When I return from repaying Charlotte, my mom greets me with "We have to get home. Now!" And we begin the complicated strategy of going home a week early. Yes, Carrie will wait a week for Jabion, to bring him to the United States for us. Yes, we can get the tickets to Thailand, Hong Kong, Chicago, and Boston. Yes, my father will not tell reporters or TV people about our arrival, except for one guy from ABC.

MAY 23, 1996

Boston. "Will Mark Pfetzer come to the front of the plane?" I know what that means. We are taxiing toward our gate at Logan. Reporters. TV people. The ABC guy must have told someone, who told someone else, and now there's a bunch of cameras waiting for me to get off the plane. The airline wants to keep them from crowding the gate, so a stewardess leads my mom and me through a back staircase to the baggage area. We see all the cameras and microphones assembled on the stairs facing the gate—away from us.

Someone spots us and the chaos begins. Lights in our eyes, cameras, microphones in our faces, shouts of "Tell us about the storm."

"Did you get hurt?" "How many died?" My short answers. My father breaks through the crowd, his head in bandages, as if he survived World War I. He looks terrible—pale, scary, his eyes tired under his white-bandaged head. He hugs my mom, then me. Hard! Strong! He's OK. I can feel it. He's going to be fine. He smiles at us. I relax, laugh, look at my mother and father; my sister, Amy, comes over, my aunt and uncle. I hug them all. More lights, other cameras, questions. Then—poof. It's over. Cameras peel away and we're alone to hoist the bags to the van.

A security guard comes up to us on the sidewalk. "Man," he says. "I've seen a lot of famous people come through, but I've never seen this many cameras." And he wishes me luck.

My father yells to me, "Check out the new license plate!" It's all numbers: 29028. The height of Mount Everest. I look at him and realize these numbers are his, too. He climbed his Everest in a Boston hospital at the same time I was climbing mine. He made it: the cancer's gone. I shake my fist at the license plate, knowing I will beat those numbers next year. I'll have the magic of the third try.

the guide

JULY 25, 1996

When I finally get on the plane for Africa, my head is spinning. Since I got home from Mount Everest six weeks ago, I have not stopped running. Literally. And now, when I sit back and think about it, it seems kind of crazy. I tried to do summer school in half the time allotted. Major papers and tests on *Julius Caesar* and *The Old Man and the Sea*, vocabulary tests, essays—I was paying for going to Everest big time. Now I sit and wonder if Brutus stabbed Hemingway's fish or Santiago was out to get Julius Caesar; it's all jumbled together because I tried to do it all in three weeks.

One night I was talking to Thor. He had a small group going to Africa. Roger Gocking was going to be the leader. Did I want to go along as assistant leader? There were a few duties for the assistant leader: answering questions, helping with logistics, offering advice. Nothing I couldn't handle. And I could climb Mount Kilimanjaro and Mount Kenya very inexpensively with Roger, one of the great guys of climbing. How could I resist?

All of a sudden, in addition to summer school, I was doing my 1,000-rep workouts, my running, nightly sit-ups, packing for Africa, telephoning climbers all over the world, and, oh yeah, getting my driver's permit. When my father took me driving in the beach parking lot, I was scared to go over five miles an hour. I can climb to 26,000 feet in a snowstorm, but this driving thing scares me.

I like driving with my father, though. He's patient; he makes it fun. He makes most things fun. Remember when you were a little kid and your father had to do an errand and you'd go—just for the ride? I can remember him sneaking me into the squad car and riding around on quiet nights. It was fun then. It's fun now. Just to be with him. We do all sorts of little things together. Go for ice cream. Go to the pistol-target range late at night, after I do my studying. Things best friends do.

He never complains about his cancer. Always the first one to do the dishes, or offer something to drink—you'd never know he'd just had a twelve-hour operation and three weeks of radiation treatments. His ear is a deep red, and inside his jaw is the jabbing pain of exposed nerves. I can only imagine how much it hurts, but he doesn't complain. He talks about it, but he doesn't complain.

What we don't talk about is how serious his condition is. Doctors tell him he's on course, that he's doing as well as could be expected, but I feel the pain with him gnawing away inside his head. Sometimes late at night, I still get the nightmare of earwigs, now grazing on the bones of Dad's inner ear, then going deeper to chomp on little pink ridges of his brain. Then I wake up and I wonder what's going on inside his head—both mentally and physically. And I wish I could do something about it.

When we're going someplace, I'll look over at him and see him wince. "I'm OK," he'll say. "I'm doing OK." Even after the daily trips to Boston for radiation—two four-minute sessions, morning and afternoon, his face in a nylon-mesh mask, the machine singing to the inside of his ear, it's still "I'm OK. Doing OK." And if he's OK, that's the way I have to be. I can't stop my climbing. He'd never hear of it. His Everest storm goes on every day, but he'd rather me call in from Africa, or Tibet, than have me sit by his side. I can feel that without him even saying it. So that's what I'll do. And do it for him.

Jabion's here for it all. I told him two years ago on my first trek to Nepal that he'd come to America. He—a mountain man, a resident of a small village of Nepal, a man of little English—didn't believe me, said, "No. You just a kid," and flashed that fluorescent smile of his. Jabion is a great Sherpa, although he's not really a Sherpa. He's a Bhotia, a different family. He's so strong that he made more trips up Everest in May than anyone, and made more bonus money as well. If the storm had not spoiled everything, I'm sure we would have summited together. That's our plan: to summit together, the sixteen-year-old American kid and the twenty-eight-year-old Nepali mountain man who became like brothers. He came home with me for the summer to study English and has become a member of our household, smiling at American supermarkets, the ocean, cable TV, the hot shower he takes every day. Now he believes me!

All this whirls through my head as I sit down for the first time in weeks without having to think of what I have to do next, or try to squeeze forty-eight hours into twenty-four—the way I've come to live my life—on purpose. I wonder who my fellow climbers—let's call them the Carletons—are. They're on this flight, a family climbing Kilimanjaro together.

Roger Gocking is from Trinidad. He has a doctorate in West African studies, runs marathons, skies 50K cross-country races, has summited many peaks over 20,000 feet, including Everest, and is a tall, skinny, gray-haired, fifty-two-year-old kid. In Nepal, where gray hair is rare, one Sherpa called him "Poppa," because Roger looked older than the Sherpa's sixty-seven-year-old father. Roger took the kidding for a couple of days, then waited for a long steep hill, gave the Sherpa a head start, and blew past him in no time. Since our Everest '95 trip together, we've talked on the phone many times, and I feel much more comfortable with him now.

I recognize the name Carleton on the ticket jacket of the woman sitting next to me. We're sitting in the middle row, and soon I'm checking out the other people she's talking to: a man, a woman, and a kid about twelve or thirteen. One thing, they're all hefty. Not fat, but definitely big. Out-of-condition big. What-are-you-doing-trying-to-climb-Kilimanjaro big. I look down the row, and the kid's chubby face, earphones, and blank stare tell me a lot about what my first climb as assistant guide will be like. This is what many people imagine "clients" are: people with enough money to do what they want. Now they want to climb a mountain, and guys like Roger and me get to help them, push them, carry them, pull them to the summit.

I think about this for a long time. I do not tell them who I am. I want the quiet so my mind's scattered pieces can connect again. I'll introduce myself later.

JULY 27, 1996

Arusha, Tanzania. Jet-lagged in a hotel room with Richard, the chubby kid, as my snoring roommate, I try to sleep. I'm staring at the ceiling and listening to CDs on my Walkman when it all hits me at once. In my half-sleep, I'm in my tent at ABC, Everest '96. First the smiling Scott Fischer comes in with his long blond hair; three-day beard; black, long-sleeved T-shirt; and green visor. Behind him is tall, coolly professional, quiet, bearded Rob Hall. We talk and joke about mountains and the people who climb them, until I realize that they are dead. Rob never saw the daughter born a few months after his death. Scott will never see his little boy and girl grow up, become my age, go to college. Scott and Rob will never see another Christmas or Fourth of July.

Why does it all devastate me here in a hotel in Africa months after the accident? I guess I had pushed my feelings to the bottom of my mind rather than feel them then. I had to survive the rest of the trip. I had so much to do after. And even now. So much to do that I haven't really thought about the deaths on Everest. But now I can think of nothing else.

All those climbers gone. Some would say foolishly, unnecessarily, irresponsibly. I disagree. Although Rob did not abide by his turnaround time and both he and Scott may have become complacent with previous success, Scott and Rob were doing their jobs helping climbers up the world's highest mountains. The job involved risks, just as my dad's job as police officer involved risks every night. If I were thirty-two years old and a doctor with a wife and kids, would I still climb? Yes, I'd have to say I would. I know how to minimize the risks. The deaths on Everest make me very sad tonight, but I know they'll have no impact on my attitude toward climbing. None whatsoever. I'll just learn from their mistakes and hope I will not be part of the parade of dead climbers that pass before a sleepless kid years from now.

JULY 30, 1996

No matter where you are on the plains of Tanzania, you see the great Mount Kilimanjaro. That's what draws so many of us climbers: at 19,340 feet, it is the highest mountain in Africa, and an accessible one at that. You cannot mistake it for any other mountain, because there are no other mountains; it stands alone, immense, snow covered, rising far above the heat of the forests and plains of northern

Tanzania, with the rounded bulk of a huge elephant dominating the landscape.

Riding through the small, scattered villages on the way to Kilimanjaro, we pass by thin, ragged people who stare out of the heat at our air-conditioned Land Rovers. Now well-fed Americans throw dust in the faces of the skinny villagers, who eat maybe once a day, who wear torn T-shirts and frayed shorts, who have no electricity or running water. Along the way, we pass women carrying large packages or water jugs balanced on their heads. They walk in a stately manner, their necks hunching and reaching to keep their balance. Imagine how tired your neck would be after walking with a gallon of water balanced on your head. Imagine walking for ten miles with ten gallons of water. That's what these women must do every day to get water for their homes. As our driver explains some points of local geography, he ignores the poverty that surrounds us, because we came here for adventure, fun, climbing—not to be concerned about such matters as the silent, scowling eyes of the people we pass. But we in the Land Rover are silently embarrassed by the contrast between ourselves and what we see outside our windows until we get closer to Kilimanjaro, where the farmland is more fertile and the villages seem livable, and we can turn down the breath of guilt in the truck.

In one village, we pass slowly under trees covered in moss so thick it looks like seaweed, then by roadside concrete slab. As we approach, I can see one man hold the head of a cow as it stands on the slab; another ties a rope around its front legs, pulls the rope, and the cow goes down, whomp, all its weight on its side. We are close to the two men and the cow, whose back legs are now flailing the air in panic. The man holding the cow's head in a half nelson yells something to the other man, who grabs a long knife, and as we pull farther away from them, I can see the man with the knife step up to the cow and slice its throat open. The other man releases the cow, and it tries to get to its hobbled knees, spewing blood in all directions, as the two men step back and watch the cow die. Just before we round a bend I can see the two men smile, the cow crumpled in death, soon probably to be in a fly-infested, unrefrigerated case in the village market.

JULY 30, 1996

When I plant my foot on the scree field that is the slope that is our trail up Kilimanjaro, I slip. I must plant each foot carefully, make firm contact; otherwise I stand on chips of rock that slide, as will I, down the mountain. Above me is the plateau that leads to the peak of Kilimanjaro—stark, brown, volcanic dirt empty of vegetation, in great contrast to the white glacier that sits parked like a huge truck on the flat surface.

It's summit day. Roger is ahead of me. Fred, the philosopher (well, almost a philosopher—almost has his doctorate), is behind him, climbing on two terrible knees, followed by the Carleton family. First there's Marion and her friend Phoebe, who are both doing well, so far. Then there's Frank, Marion's husband, whose red face and slow pace seem to ask that eternal question "What the hell am I doing up here?" and Richard, Marion's son from her first marriage, who is still sitting far down the slope—not moving.

Roger yells down to Richard, "What's the problem?"

Richard yells back, "Have to go to the bathroom so bad I can't move."

Dr. Roger, college professor, the guide and mountain authority, comes up with an unique suggestion, "Well, go."

"Don't have any toilet paper."

So Roger, the leader, carefully makes his way down the scree to bring little Richard some toilet paper and returns, rolling his eyes.

(Roger rolls his eyes often about Richard. We both do. Richard inspires a lot of eye rolls. He couldn't help put up the tent—didn't know how. He can't help with anything—doesn't know how.)

Richard is still sitting in the same place. "Richard," his stepfather yells, "we're waiting." Bad enough, I suppose, to have the whole crew, including the African guides and workers, watching from a distance, waiting for him to take a dump so we can continue.

"I can't go! It's too cold."

And that was Richard the whole trip—just sitting there with his Walkman blasting rap through his earphones, eyes shut, sprawled. His mother said Richard aspired to his biological father's philosophy: Never stand if you can sit; never sit when you can lie down.

After dinner one night, there was one incredible moment of natural beauty that seemed to last for twenty minutes. Our campsite faced the western wall leading to the peak of Kilimanjaro. Brilliant golds and reds inflamed the wall from the fire of the setting sun. Just above the mountain's plateau, the full moon sat against the blue sky as if it were a cue ball on the tabletop plateau. The colors and light seemed to be suspended in time. There was no sound except for the murmur of after-dinner cleanup. I stood for fifteen minutes, probably with my mouth open, taking in every angle.

Not Richard. The little creep was in his tent, on his sleeping bag, earphones cranked up, staring at the ceiling. I wanted to shake him, pound his head, something, to wake him up! But I couldn't. I am, after all, only the assistant guide. So I have to listen to his tedious talk. How he's "almost up to solid C's" on his report card. C's? That's supposed to be good? How he'd yell, "Mark, wait for me." And I'd wait while this thirteen-year-old had to rest. (I tried to teach him pace—to move efficiently without tiring too quickly. He eventually was able to do an hour without a break.)

Once up the scree field, his stepfather asks him to carry a water jug. "F— you! Carry it yourself!" Richard yells back. Frank looks back at him and says nothing.

Whoa! I'm standing in the brilliant sunshine of Kilimanjaro doing what I love to do best, and it's as if this kid just slugged me in the face. Richard is me three years earlier. Only he'd never be me. Never will be. At thirteen I ached so to be on some mountain adventure, I went out and raised the money and trekked through Nepal because I wanted to know I could, and here I am this kid's guide. Same age I was. He's content to let someone bring him toilet paper, to get C's, to shrug off the most beautiful natural scene so he can listen to rap and stare at the walls of his tent, and I want to shake him till his eyes roll and tell him to get a focus to his life, there's so much to do and see and be.

And I want to put my fist in his face and scream at him, "Don't you ever talk to your stepfather like that!" I think of my father and how he fights every day and says he's OK, and how he helps me so much and puts his arm around me—even now. Besides, my father would kill me if I ever said that to him.

The moment passes. The stepfather picks up the water jug but, defeated by the steep scree, the altitude, his poor conditioning, and, no doubt, Richard's swearing at him, decides to go back down to camp. Fred, the philosopher; August, an African guide; and I summit. Soon Roger, Marion, Phoebe, and Richard follow us. Looking out over the plains of Africa with its patches of dark green fifty miles away, I am on a summit like no other. Beneath us is the wildlife of the plains; next to me is a glacier the size of a huge convention center; behind us is a volcano.

As a guide, I feel strange about my new responsibilities. Marion does not want to return the way we came, down the steep and somewhat difficult scree field. She insists that, despite Roger's advice, she, Phoebe, and Richard will traverse a portion of Kilimanjaro and descend a far easier route. Roger tries to persuade, then orders them to go with us, but they take Daniel, an African guide, who has no choice but to take them on their own route. There is nothing we can do.

On the way down from the summit, August asks politely if I'd like to go first. Not thinking, I say, "Sure." Fred follows me, and August follows him, with Roger trailing behind. Soon I realize why August didn't want to go first, as scree stones and rocks fly by my head. They are dislodged by Fred and August as they descend. First one down becomes a target. I have no choice but to take gigantic steps to get out of their range. My feet sink into the shale, and then I spring back out and soon I'm down, ahead of August and Fred and their rocks.

I know I was supposed to be the guide here, but Richard taught me a lot. He taught me how lucky I am. He taught me that a thirteen-year-old without focus or direction can have a tough time of it. His parents can give him so much—including an easy way down the mountain, but he's got to want to make it himself. No matter what they do, it's up to him to put down the rap music and claim his own life.

AUGUST 5, 1996

Hiking in Mount Kenya National Park was tense, an adventure far beyond the sixteen miles of hilly terrain we encountered. What made it tense was the presence of Cape buffalo, as big an animal as it sounds, an animal that likes, more than any other animal does, to stalk, attack, and kill humans. In two days of hiking, we saw signs of Cape buffalo, but none up close.

Passing through a village of the Masai warriors this morning, those tall guys who still wear cloths and carry spears, I see the meanest-looking guy I've ever seen in my life, more intimidating than the biggest Cape buffalo could ever be. He's about seven feet tall and his eyes are red-rimmed and crazy, his face caked with a clay makeup, his hair slicked back with a red clay stuck all the way through it. He's wearing the traditional dark red Masai robe, or cloth, wound around his skinny torso, and in one hand carries a spear that you know has to be razor sharp, just looking at the guy's eyes. In the other, he has a little club with a ball on its end. The ball has little sharp objects sticking out, guaranteed to cause pain. When the Masai kill an animal, they like to make sure they preserve all its blood so they can drink it later. This guy looks like he just had his morning drink of blood, and he's looking at me as if he knows mine would be a nice treat later. Do I take his picture? Do I even get my camera out? No. I offer a friendly smile and a nod and ever so carefully retreat back to the Land Rover, as if I've encountered a lion rather than another human being.

That's what Kenya's like for us. Hiking in Mount Kenya National Park, where Masai stalk game and Cape buffalo stalk humans and kill them.

CHAPTER SIXTEEN cho oyu

AUGUST 28, 1996

I'm sitting in the back of the truck as it lurches up the belt of mud that hugs the side of the Tibetan mountains. I'm not sitting, really; I'm straddling the back panel, ready to jump if the truck goes over the edge, which I'm certain will happen at every turn the truck makes. The gears whine; we jolt and slide from side to side, and we search each other's faces in the pale light for signs of fear, nervousness, or panic. Obviously, climbers, including me, have a drive for danger. I will also claim a sense of caution within that danger. That's why I have one foot over the back panel, ready to jump if I have to.

On our way to take on Cho Oyu—one of the ten highest mountains in the world, on the Nepal-Tibet border—we are on a roller-coaster ride in a heavy, monsoon downpour, on steep, muddy mountain roads with 2,000-foot drops, in the body of a truck piled with bags of gear and people, covered with tarpaulin because of the rain. It's crowded and, worse, dark, because the rain drumming on the tarp won't allow us to see out. To tell the truth, we're in a lot of danger riding in the back of this truck. But we climbers love being here, choose to be here, pay to be here! It's fun!

During a break, forced by rocks on the road, Henry Todd, our expedition leader, comes to our truck with an option. "The road above is very bad," he warns. "There's a truck going up. I don't recommend taking it because of the rocks falling. Walking will be safer." We don't think dodging rocks on foot is safer, so we all get on the truck. The mud's so bad a bulldozer has to pull us up the steep mud, but we make it. The situation reminds me of Africa. Roger Gocking and I were stranded because a worker put a forklift through the fuselage of our plane as it sat in the Dar es Salaam airport. The only flight available was on Air Madagascar. A lot of people refused to get on a plane from Air Madagascar, which they imagined could only be rickety. We went and had a great flight on a brand-new 747.

Next to me is Paul Fletcher, a friend from home, on his first expedition. You can tell he's new because he's got both feet over the back panel. He's learning that out here in the mountains you have to be flexible—things don't always go according to plan. In fact, they seldom do. So you adapt the Sherpa attitude: "No problem. Maybe yes. Maybe no." You just have to wait. For example, we got to customs at Zhangmu this morning at eleven or so. "Sorry. Lunch," the guard says. And what would have been a fifteen-minute border crossing becomes a three-hour wait. Or be prepared for mud, downpours, fine mist, and humidity. That's what expeditions are all about: the hassles of getting there, the stories of unexpected adventures. You always remember the summits, but riding in the back of a truck on rain-slicked mud inches away from a long drop-off becomes equally etched in your mind.

What am I doing back in Tibet, a few months after Everest? Why go through the same old rituals of long flights and days of travel so soon? Good questions. Since Everest, I've been on a roll. I managed to do summer school in half the allotted time. By late July, I was off to Mount Kilimanjaro and Mount Kenya, then to Salt Lake City for the annual mountain-equipment trade show to meet with potential sponsors. I flew back to New York for a TV show with Michael Jordan's mom, young Olympic heroes and their parents, my mom and me. The next day I flew back out west to the Grand Tetons and finally, from there, straight to the Boston airport to meet Jabion and Paul for our expedition to Cho Oyu.

My father still has no signs of any more cancer, and the doctor hopes to control the terrible pain in his jaw through medication. But, I must admit, I worry. I don't say much, and when people ask, I always say he's doing very well. I watch him very closely, to see what chemotherapy does to him, to see him so skinny his pants are baggy, to see him hold the side of his face as if it were a bomb ready to go off at any time. I know the chemo and medication are all part of the program, which is supposed to make sure he'll stay cancer-free, and I know the doctor says the pain will subside once the nerves in the jaw calm down. I watch my mother, always calm, always cheerful, as if the whole problem were only a minor, temporary toothache. Mom always bustles around taking charge; I'm always getting ready to go on some trip; Dad's always taking his medication; but, in bed, late at night, I know the what we all think about: the weeks go by and the invisible cancer ticks away beneath the surface. I tell no one of my thoughts. I will not be an enemy to all the positive feelings about Dad's cancer. But the thoughts are there, every day, every night, as if a small cell of his cancer found a place to grow in my head. Now I must control the thoughts, same as I control the thoughts of panic in a tough spot on a climb. I will trust the equipment, move forward, and focus on each small step.

I came to Cho Oyu so soon because of Everest '97. That's my focus. This expedition presents a great opportunity to climb Cho Oyu for its own sake. But everything I do this year will be for the purpose of Everest '97. The 26,750-foot Cho Oyu—8,153 meters high—will provide a very good test of my skills. (Only fourteen peaks in the world are over 8,000 meters high—always measured, by the way, in the internationally recognized metric system.) I know I will be ready next May. I'm so sure, I quit school to prepare for the magic of the third try.

I should say I'm staying out of school for a year. Now that I'm sixteen, I can do that legally. I want to focus on training, climbing, and tracking down sponsors. I also want to do well academically, and I know that school is more than keeping up with assignments while I'm sitting in a base camp somewhere. The way I'm trying to go through school will hurt me in the long run. I have to learn to write, and think, and develop ideas, so I can get into college and med school. The only way I can really improve is to be in school. I realize I can't prepare well for my academic future and prepare for Everest at the same time. So instead of lugging books halfway around the world, trying to keep up with my "work," I'll just stay away and go back full-time next year. I thought about it very carefully. I will lose a year, not graduate with my class, but Everest '97 will be well worth the sacrifice.

Besides, I won't lose that much socially, because I never had much of a "normal" teenage existence. Ask me how many dates I've had and I'll tell you the truth: zero. I still don't feel that comfortable around people my own age. Especially girls. As if I've already gone beyond being a teenager without experiencing it. Maybe I'm self-conscious, maybe I feel funny trying to explain what I do, because I know they won't really understand. I'm polite. I smile. I try to do well in school. If I'm not there now, it's because I'm where I'd rather be—on a mountain somewhere.

The truck bangs around another curve, throwing us against each other in the gloomy dark. Paul has the look I must have had on my first trip here, the "what-have-I-got-myself-into" look. He's already had his introduction to Tibet life: packs of howling dogs roaming all night outside our hotel; a dog walking into our room to lift its leg and pee on the wall; a few days later, in another hotel, a cow deciding to come into our room to say hello. Then we went to a restaurant and what's on the menu? Dog. But Paul's ready. I can tell. At our last stop, he got down from the truck, and all the road workers muttered, "Rambo." No wonder. He wears a tank top, fatigue pants, and a bandanna around his forehead. And he's got more muscles than Sylvester Stallone. Used to own a gym. Lifts weights. Runs. In great shape. Is he ready for high-altitude climbing? That's the big question. He's only been into rock-gym and New England climbing so far. Rambo's ready to give it a try.

Our other expedition members are bouncing around back here, too. Larry's over in the corner, wearing the baseball cap his teenage daughters gave him to wear on summit day. Larry's a forty-year-old lawyer from Chicago, who, for some reason, has vowed never to introduce me to his daughters, says he loves them too much. Larry made himself into a very big hero a couple of days ago. We were hiking in Tibet and stopped for water. Henry, Paul, Larry, and I sat on a grassy ridge fantasizing about food. Paul and I do it all the time in restaurants. Rather than the dog we're really eating, we decide it's chicken cordon bleu or steak flambé we're eating. Somehow, maybe it was Larry who started it, we were talking bagels. Warm, soft, fresh bagels. Larry, reaching into his backpack, said, "Would this help?" and, as if by magic, pulled out two blueberry bagels he'd brought from Chicago. He'd saved them for over a week, resisted the temptation to eat them, and there we sat, eating Chicago bagels on a Tibetan hillside. We each ate a half, very slowly. They were wonderful.

Next to Larry, hanging on to each other as they slide around on the gear, are Keith and Chris, a married couple. Keith is an affluent architect from Georgia in his early fifties. Chris is in her late twenties, in excellent condition, and looks it. Pavel is over on the other side, jammed in between two guys from another expedition. Pavel is from Poland, but works in chemicals in South Africa. He's rail-thin, six feet six, and stays to himself. He told me once, "You know, I've never littered. So one day I'm in the car, and I throw a Coke can out the window. It felt so good." Strange guy.

Ray Dorr and Anatoli Broukeev, the other members of our small group, aren't here yet. But our Sherpas are: Pemba, our cook; Ang Tshering; and, of course, Jabion. All ready to go. Provided, of course, we survive our trial by mud, rain, heat, and mountain truck.

SEPTEMBER 8, 1996

Advanced Base Camp. The perfect spot for my tent has one problem: a rock right where I want my tent floor to go. Very important to find the right spot. Like going to the beach. Ever watch people set up at the beach? All kinds of room on the sand, and they have to spend ten minutes finding the exact spot for their blanket. I'm like that at Advanced Base Camp; you have a beautiful view of the mountain all the way up to the summit, and all the way down to Chinese Base Camp, on an area flat enough to be our home for the next week. So, sure, I'm going to be a little picky about my tent spot—close enough to the others but separate enough to give me a little privacy. Am I going to move my tent? No. Not me. I'm going to move the rock.

Paul comes by, gasping for breath from the altitude, takes a look at me digging around a buried rock as if it were some treasure chest full of diamonds, and asks the simple question: "Why?"

"It's in the way, that's why. And don't tell me to move my tent, because I'm not gonna do it!"

This is a prime tent spot. I put my back to the rock, and it inches forward. I strain against it again—the thing must be three hundred pounds—and now *I'm* gasping for air. The hell with it. Stupid thing to do, anyway, dig out a rock. Paul walks away. I get out tent poles, start to unroll my tent to set up some other place. Then, I can't help myself, I'm back at it, digging my way around the buried part of the rock. People going by—Sherpas, climbers—stop to watch the American kid waste all his energy at ABC digging out a rock. Some offer suggestions; others roll their eyes and walk away.

For three hours of outrageous puffing, I dig at this stubborn, ugly, dirt-covered, magnified, petrified wart. Why? I don't know why! But I have to do it. After a while, other guys start to help me. Slowly it surrenders its hole, and we roll it down near the trail. I thank everyone, sit on the rock regaining my breath, and look off into the sky now streaked with deep, late-day clouds. From here I can look two miles directly across the valleys of glacier ice at Nangpa La, the pass that leads from Nepal into Tibet. I can see dots inching their way along, and I know they are members of climbing expeditions heading out for other Himalayan peaks, doing what we're doing. Next spring, a similar expedition will come up here and a climber will look at the huge wart-rock in the middle of the trail and ask, "Where'd this come from?" And no one will be able to come up with a logical answer. Except for me. I needed my tent spot.

The French need their spots as well. Which must explain why they set up in between our tents. Space is becoming limited at ABC now, that's for sure. But they have to be right on top of us, like obnoxious suntanners who put their blankets an inch away. And they smoke! At Advanced Base Camp! They also strip right down and bathe naked, right on the trail. People pass—men, women—these French guys don't care.

Coming up to ABC was an unusual adventure. I thought going

through the Khumbu Icefall to get to Camp One on Everest was roulette climbing. Here, we have no pieces of falling ice to duck, just real bullets. The Chinese Base Camp, as it's called, is right on the Nepal-Tibet border. The Tibet border patrol has a post near the Base Camp. In fact, you have to go through an area close to the post as you leave Base Camp for Camp One, an area the border guards are quick to patrol. The trouble is these guys love to shoot and are quick to use their rifles. Ask Russell Brice; he was shot at as he came down to Base Camp last week. But all you have to do is wave your hats and let them know that you're friendly, or so Russell says.

So that's what we did as we climbed to ABC. As we rounded the corner of the trail near the border post, we waved our hats like madmen. If they started to shoot, we figured we'd just send Paul up there. He still has his "Rambo" image going for him. He'd wipe 'em out. They'd all run for their lives, even though our only weapons were the ski poles we walked with.

Heavy-duty waving seemed to work. Once past the border patrol, the next challenge was the scree slope that led to Camp One. Scree, as we've seen before, is slippery, small stones, in this case on a very steep part of the mountain. Hiking on it is like trying to walk in deep, soft sand at a very steep angle. At altitude, it can quickly turn the most fit people into Jell-O. Best way for me to handle it was to put Jimi Hendrix on my Walkman, listen to the worst version of the national anthem ever recorded, and grind it out.

Acclimatizing is coming along slowly. Digging a tent platform in the snow at Camp One made me light-headed, as did the scree climb, but now at ABC I'm much better. Even fighting with the rock helped me acclimatize. I was concerned to watch Jabion struggle more than most of us. He'd been at my parents' house at sea level for six weeks, leading the soft American life. His body probably liked it, got used to it, didn't want to go back to work. It didn't help that he had some food poisoning on the way to Base Camp. I've never seen Jabion in a situation before where I had to go back and help him with his backpack because he wasn't up to carrying it. He's getting stronger all the time, but he's far from the Jabion I've always known.

Watching Jabion, Paul, Russell, and Anatoli, who joined us last night, I can see firsthand what the body can do in difficult situations. Paul is in great shape by any standards. Up here at ABC and higher, though, he's struggling to keep up. Needs to find his own pace. He's not eating well; he's losing weight, energy's down, cough's developing, but he's still progressing because he's tough. Have to be when a hit-and-run motorcycle accident leaves you with two broken legs and a shredded face at eighteen. He came back from that to run, lift, and ski. The other day, Henry asked him if he knew how to rappel. Paul was facing a short ice cliff at the time, and he had no choice but to say, "No, but I'd like to learn." Which he did. On a cliff, high in the Himalayas, with a 5,000-foot drop if he made any errors.

I was climbing an ice face with Russell two days ago. (Russell is actually a member of a different team, but the word *team* tends to lose its meaning on mountain climbs. Technically, Russell's "team" only shares the permit cost with our "team." Two distinct groups of climbers, maybe, but in reality we climb together all the time.) I was creeping up the steep face, digging crampons in, sliding my jumar up the rope, getting there. I looked up at Russell jumaring his way up the ice face in no time, stabbing the ice with each foot: a fury of high-speed climbing. Although there was nothing to stop a very long fall, he was ice climbing as if it were a little frozen waterfall off an interstate in New York. How'd he do that?

Or Anatoli? He had been home for his father's unexpected funeral. No climbing of any kind for six weeks. Comes back here and joins us at ABC with no acclimatizing at all. Just shows up, unacclimated, untrained, and says he's ready to climb. This is the same Anatoli who, in May, went out three or four times into the dark of that ice-laden, 100-mph wind on Everest, and each time came back with climbers. His body must always be ready—maybe it's all that speck he eats.

Climbing to Camp One, I started to wonder if I'd be strong enough to summit. No workouts with Nel this time. No real training for some time. At least I wasn't the M&M's man. Al Burgess told me about one of his clients who was a taste tester for M&M's. Pathetic climber. Had to put him on a yak to get him moving, even on a trekking trip.

As we came up to ABC, I noticed I was getting stronger, breathing easier—the main problem someone like Paul must be having. When you are first at altitude, you feel like you're suffocating, and you want to rip away your hood and anything around your face—goggles, ski mask, anything restricting. There is nothing more scary than being suffocated.

SEPTEMBER 11, 1996

Dinner at ABC is much more relaxed than some expeditions I've been on. Pavel is an easy target for guys like Ray and Keith, but he takes it well. This afternoon, we were fixing rope up to Camp Two. Pavel had gone up ahead of us, unroped, exploring on his own as usual. As he came down toward us in those long, gawky strides of his, he was heading straight for a crevasse, which he couldn't see because of the angle of the slope. We were all waving and yelling at him to stop. He was waving back, smiling, and striding right along. Henry finally bellowed as only Henry can, and Pavel stopped two feet from a surprise descent.

Ray and Keith are giving Pavel grief about paying attention, about how lucky he was that Henry's there to watch over him. Ray says, "Yeah. Not like some leaders who only pay attention to their girlfriends. Right, Mark?"

Keith jumps right in. "Don't you get on Thor's case. The guy makes one mistake, and you'd think he was a criminal. He's a great climber." Keith's face is getting red. He's been on expeditions with Thor many times. "And he runs a very good program!"

"Good program?" Ray says. "Were you on Everest last year? He screwed up big time."

They both turn to me. I was on Everest with Thor. Everyone at the table knows that. *I'm* supposed to settle the argument? I have no intention of getting into it. "Look," I say, "Thor's a great climber, a great guy. He's a friend of mine and a good climbing partner." Keith and Ray wait for me to say something else, to agree with one side or the other. But I don't. Everest '95's over. No point holding grudges against a good friend.

We change the subject to the Koreans who were hang-gliding from Camp Two, and the Russian climber who passed us with a snowboard, and Russell, who intends to ski from the summit. And soon the table is laughing again at the absurd measures climbers will go to try something new.

We talk about summit day, still a few days off but now in our sights. "Is easy mountain for you, Mark. You can climb. No problem," says Anatoli. For him everything seems easy. At Base Camp one day, in Camp Two looking for a place to sleep the next. Then with us up to Camp Three. No problem. Call it the Anatoli Acclimatization Technique, meaning there *is* no acclimatization. The thin air that's sucking the energy out of Rambo Paul has no negative impact on skinny, gold-toothed Anatoli. Hardly seems human, but it shows how a body gets used to responding, instinctively, to the repeated demands of thin-air living. Anatoli's probably like Reinhold Messner—nothing truly unique about their lung capacities or musculatures to indicate superior physical attributes, only a great sense of will. Messner called it the deciding factor. "Not strength," he said, "but will. Will makes the body go up like an arrow."

That's certainly true in Anatoli's case. Paul told me this morning that Anatoli was watching me climb. He said I was so much stronger than he saw me at Everest. That's good to hear.

SEPTEMBER 16, 1996

Summit day. Two A.M. Organization is the key to success on summit day. Organization and attention to detail—without them you could make the one little mistake that could cost you fingers, toes, your life. You start the night before by organizing every aspect of your equipment. Have it all set up in neat piles so that you can be ready very quickly: there's nothing worse than disrespecting your climbing partners by being late; besides, no one will stand outside your tent and wait for you in the three A.M. cold. By that time I want to know that every knot is doubled, that every aspect of my equipment is ready. I even have a big question mark on each glove to remind me to question everything. Otherwise, at three A.M., when the mind is already fuzzy with sleep and altitude, I'd have no way to keep check.

Oxygen is one thing I won't have to worry about, either carrying it or using it. Jabion and I have decided to join most of the others and summit without any supplementary oxygen. If you are in good shape and can climb well, I feel you don't really need oxygen. Even if you are only sixteen. Even at 27,000 feet; even above the Death Zone. In fact, if you carry the equipment—mask and canisters—then you're going to need to use oxygen just to deal with the extra weight. That's the theory, anyway.

I have another theory as well: young climbers—kids my age,

maybe younger—can climb better than older climbers, because we can recover faster. Younger climbers don't need as much rest between camps, don't tire as easily. Therefore, we lower the opportunity for illness and weather problems by reducing our overall time on the high mountains. Once we learn to pace ourselves properly—being careful to use our energy efficiently—I think we have the potential to be much stronger than, and maybe as successful as, older climbers. Though older climbers do have the mental toughness only experience can give.

At 2:30 A.M., you've struggled into your layers of clothes, even put on sunscreen (when the sun comes up you'll be too busy to remember), and now you have the opportunity for an aerobic workout: putting on your shoes. You're not even pumped up about summiting, because all your attention is focused on your feet! Liners, soft inner boots, hard-shell outer boots, rubber supergaiters, neoprene overboots, and crampons. Each put on while you're sitting on the floor of your tent, struggling as if you were trying to put pants on over ski boots. By 2:45 A.M., you feel you've grunted, groaned, and wasted away much of your energy, and you haven't even left your tent!

Pavel decided last night he'd had enough. He stayed at Camp Two, saying that climbing was like a blind date—you never know what you're going to get. I guess the date didn't work out very well for him.

A greater surprise is Paul. At the last minute, he decides not to go. He comes out of his tent, drained, exhausted from his efforts to get to 24,000 feet. The altitude has eaten away at his appetite, energy, and muscle mass so that he's now so weak, he has no Rambo left for the final push.

Henry shouts at him, tries to get him going. "You didn't come all this way to stop here! You're coming up with me."

Paul shakes his head no, admitting defeat. Henry mutters to

himself and takes off up the trail, alone. I want to tell Paul that he's gone a great deal higher than most experienced climbers have done on their first high-altitude climbs. But there's no sense telling him that now. It's not the time for conversation.

Soon we're up to the snowbank near the rock band. The icy moon shines on the rock as we jumar up the twelve feet, then as the black begins to drain from the sky, we are on the hard-packed snow, traversing back and forth in switchbacks because of the deep angle of the slope. I love the feeling of patient, steady progress, the strength in my legs, the crunch of snow, even the challenge of breathing so high up—which, so far, is manageable. But no matter how warmly dressed, I have trouble with the cold. Suppose you're in a plane, going to the West Coast, say, and you're cruising along at 28,000 feet, watching a movie or reading. You look out the window and you see a little thermometer. It would read between 45 and 60 below. We're at 26,000 feet, and it's at least 25 below, with an increasing wind. The higher we go, the colder it'll be.

Despite the cold, Chris, Larry, Keith, Henry, Russell, and I are moving ahead of the others up the switchbacks, the route we've planned. A route is like developing a map of an unknown territory, then following the map to get through it. What keeps us coming back to the mountains, I think, is this unknown part.

I've learned that whenever you plan an expedition you rely on books, experienced climbers in the group, word of mouth from other climbers, and the skill level of the group to determine your route. Routes are not at all precise. They deal with broad areas. You might aim for a particular rock face or gully, which leads to a ridge you have to cross. You have to consider the location of camps, too, which are more specific, because they offer safety, protection. But, no matter how well you plan a route, you never know what's ahead of you. So you have to adjust—constantly.

That's the fun of it, coming up with solutions to problems that jump up, such as now, getting through an area of steep rocks covered by light, loose snow. The ice ax won't dig in, crampons slip, and, unroped as we are, we can see the whole mountain below us in a huge drop-off: the sort of scene that could send someone into a frozen panic. Experience keeps me calm and lets me figure out that I'll make it, that I can even enjoy this little problem, if I'm patient enough to work through it.

Up to a snowfield, then to a platform about a half-mile from the summit. The wind by now has whipped at us from all angles on the switchbacks, and I'm thinking about air. All this open space and wind, yet so little air to breathe. There's enough, though. Enough to take four shallow breaths for every step. I can feel my heart and lungs working like crazy, but they're OK, engines revved up to the max, pumping my legs slowly through the wind to the top. The biggest problem this high without oxygen, despite my good pace, is my oxygen-deprived, slow-motion brain. Chris is right behind me as we head to the summit, the two youngest keeping the strongest pace, except for Russell, of course, who passes us at will. If Chris were to ask me something simple right now, say to add 9 and 8, I'd be able to tell her—in about a minute. I just hope nothing complicated comes up. I'd be overwhelmed. And so would she. Everything now is filtered through this sense of slow-brain, and I must pay close attention to everything I do.

I wait for Jabion to catch up to us, and we summit together. An adrenaline rush pushes me the last few steps, and we are here. Jabion and I hug, give slow-motion high-fives. It is Jabion's third trip to Cho Oyu. He's so happy finally to summit.

I kneel down to rest. From here I can see across to Everest, and Lhotse looming huge, close. I can see Everest's South Col, West Ridge, Western Cwm, all the views you see in photographs, and get a sense of where I am. I am at the *summit* of an 8,000-meter peak, 26,750 feet up! On Everest, I was nearly as high, but not on a summit. I'm the youngest ever to summit a peak this high!

My mountain hack chooses right now to kick into high coughing gear. As Chris asks me to look up from my kneeling position for a photo, I start coughing so hard I get the dry heaves. No food in my system and very thin air combine to send me to all fours for a wonderful photo of the conquering hero. But, overall, I'm very satisfied to be here: proof that my theory works. All the trips up and down from ABC to Camps One and Two, all the care to proper pace and attention to detail, demonstrate that a well-trained young person can do well on 8,000-meter peaks—even without oxygen. I sneak another look over at Everest. That's the thing: I'm looking across, almost at the same height, it seems, parallel. And I earned my way up here, without oxygen, on strong legs, with enough energy left, I'm convinced, to climb the 2,000 more feet to Everest's summit. Even from here, on all fours, my stomach roiling from dry heaves, I can envision a route up the South Col, to Camp Four, to the top.

I recover quickly enough for a photo with Jabion. While we're posing, Russell readies his skies to try a run from the summit. "Too bad you didn't beat that eleven-year-old kid who was up here yesterday," he jokes. So much for respect from my peers.

Jabion, Chris, and I start down, as Russell tries to ski. He's an excellent skier, but his climbing boots are so awkward on skies, he falls as much as I would. We pass Ray, Henry, and Larry, who are almost to the top now. I know how they're feeling. They're struggling, gasping, looking for that last bit of energy to make it to the top, and they meet us coming down with Jabion-type smiles on our faces. We look at them and say, "Just a little farther," as Russell swooshes by on his skies.

The importance of attention to detail: as we descend, Keith, who is behind us, suddenly shouts, "Chris! My glove! Get my glove!" But it's too late. We see, flying down past us, scurrying like a black little animal on the snow, Keith's heavy mitten. Keith's an enthusiastic, energetic guy who loves to climb. He's away from his architectural business so often, he gave his partner a BMW convertible, out of guilt, I guess. But he's not always attentive to detail. This time he'd forgotten to use his idiot straps—the ones that go around your wrists so you can take off the outer mittens to untie a rope and not lose them—and the mitten escaped. "Chris! Can you see it?"

"No, I can't see it! What do you want me to do?" Chris gives it right back to him. Keith doesn't say another word. It's warm enough on the way down that he'll get no frostbite, but imagine if he were near the summit and he had to take off his heavy mittens to tie a knot, as can so often happen. Sure, he'd have his Thinsulate gloves on, but the loss of a heavy mitten, dropped because he'd forgotten to pay attention to the idiot straps, would soon cost him the use of his hand, and eventually his life.

On the way to Camp Three, the sun is high, the wind drops, and suddenly it is very warm. Henry had said not to bother carrying our heavy down suits, just to wear them. Good thing I didn't listen to him. Sure, it's easier to just keep going in the down suit, but it is increasingly hot, raising the dehydration problem. Reminds me of the climbers on Aconcagua who were coming up in down suits, while the rest of us were in T-shirts. One almost died of dehydration. Attention to detail.

I'm glad I planned to take mine off. No disrespect to Henry. He's a very good leader, but he has his own beliefs. Paul obeyed Henry's advice about Diamox, a diuretic we take to help acclimatize. Too much Diamox and you constantly urinate away all your nutrients, a problem that could have had an impact on Paul's low energy level. Maybe I've finally learned how to deal with expedition leaders—

always listen to their advice, but let your own experience and knowledge of yourself be the boss.

By two P.M., we're back at Camp Three. I'm not done, not that tired. I want to go on to Camp Two. I always want to push to get down as low as possible after I summit, for the reward of warmer, more breathable air. By the time I get to Camp Two, I have used so many calories I'm shivering with cold. I'm hoping Paul will be there with pots on the stove and something hot to drink. But our tent is empty. And, while I have to go through the ritual of melting snow for water and food and have no one to talk to, I find I enjoy the freedom of movement, the eventual warm rice and tea, the comfort of a sleeping bag, and the deep, sweet, sleep to be a wonderful celebration of my first 8,000-meter summit.

SEPTEMBER 17, 1996

The long walk down to Base Camp is anything but lonely. It's so good to meet climbers coming up, people you know from other teams, who look at your dirty, ragged condition and the smile you can't keep from your face and congratulate you. Then in Base Camp, Pavel comes out, then Paul with his camera, and later Russell invites us all to his tent for a feast of meat dumplings, eel, rice, yak meat, and all the Mars bars Paul and I can eat.

SEPTEMBER 22, 1996

Elizabeth Hawley finds our team in our hotel in Kathmandu. She's the most important media figure in Kathmandu's climbing community. At one time she was Sir Edmund Hillary's secretary. Over the last twenty years, Liz has made it a practice to track down every expedition, take notes from every climber about each Himalayan climb, and report significant mountaineering events to the world. In the process she's become kind of a historian of Himalayan climbing.

She asks the group questions, takes notes about us, about our route, our weather, the time our summit bid took. She looks at me. "As far as I can tell, you are the youngest to summit an 8,000-meter peak." The others nod. No standing ovation, no applause. Just a nod of acknowledgment. No big deal. To them or me. We're all climbers together; I just happen to be younger.

More important is next May, Cho Oyu as a giant step toward the summit of Everest. On the summit of Cho Oyu I felt strong, healthy, and capable. I'm learning, always learning: about attention to details, about pace, about making my own decisions, about what I must do until next March, when I'll get on a plane for Kathmandu and the magic of the third try. The next few months will only make me better.

the decision

NOVEMBER 22, 1996

*M*ark's grandfather says it's important for him to get home as soon as possible!" I jump up from the campfire and strain to see who's yelling across the night-dark river. It's Chuck's friend, the man who owns the land where we're camping in rural Pennsylvania. It's past ten on this cold November night, and the man would not normally be out this way in his truck unless it was an emergency. Must be Dad, his jaw so painful lately he just sits and rocks, even with full medication.

I am very worried now, scared. I try the cell phone. Won't work. Chuck drives me to a small-town pay phone. I call Massachusetts Eye and Ear Hospital. Dad's not there. Where else would he be? He was fine two days ago, home. Neurologist had him perform eye movements, face squeezes, winks. Everything fine. That night we went out to dinner. He laughed, ate well. The next morning Chuck and I started on this camping trip we've planned for a long time. I ask for the telephone number of Massachusetts General, adjoining

Eye and Ear. They don't know the number. "What!" I scream. "How can you not know the number? I have to find my father!" I slam the phone down.

Where is he? I want to talk to my mother; she'll give me a straight answer. I reluctantly call my grandfather. I don't want to talk to him; I need to talk to my mom. How fast can I be there, he wants to know. I want to talk to my mother, I tell him. He gives me a number. My fingers are too nervous to dial. Chuck gets Mass. General's ICU, gives me the phone.

I finally get my mother. My father's being worked on; they got most of the cancer out of his brain. Can go no further, otherwise risk paralysis of the whole right side of his body. In the two days since I left, his eye began to droop, his smile began to twist, so an operation was scheduled to remove the joint in his jaw to relieve pain. That's when the doctors learned the cancer had spread to his brain. I want to hitchhike to Pittsburgh, get a flight to Boston, see him, touch him. No, my mother says. Come home tomorrow with Chuck. There's nothing anyone can do.

Nothing anyone can do. The doctors are doing everything possible. Does she know how those words frustrate me? How I feel when I watch him sitting at the kitchen table, rocking and saying, "I hope I'm not going to die from this." And my mother and father both sit there and cry. I don't know what to do but go into my room, shut the door, and pull the pillow over my head so no one can hear me. That's what I did last night. Went off into the woods alone and cried. I can climb the highest mountains in the world and do, it seems, whatever I set my mind to. So why can't I help him?

NOVEMBER 24, 1996

Paul Fletcher drives me to Boston as soon as I get home. It's almost midnight when I finally see my father. He's hooked up, medicated, asleep. But Mom tells me he'll have less pain now that they removed what was left of his jawbone. The right side of his face will be paralyzed, and they'll have to put a gold weight in his eyelid so it can close. But so what? He's still my dad, still the same guy, and he'll be out of here cracking those jokes of his in a few days.

I go out into the hallway and look at the Boston night outside the huge windows. The cancer's still there, been there the whole time. MRIs didn't pick it up because of scar tissue from the first operation, which hid the cancer from the MRIs and let us think he was cancer-free. He'll have more chemotherapy. There'll be no guarantee, no talk of cure: they will try to prevent the cancer from spreading any farther. That's what it will be for now. Containment. Small steps. Like climbing that narrow ledge on Ama Dablam. No panic. If we just focus on each careful step, we will make it. I know we will.

NOVEMBER 26, 1996

An elementary school basement, rows of chairs, a screen, slide projector, tables full of climbing equipment: I'm ready for another slide show. But this one's different. It's sponsored by the Middletown School Department. Administration people, school committee people, and the curious public file in to see the slides of the kid who went to Everest. I've gone over my slides again and again, got a haircut, have on a tie and, I bet, a look of surprise at the great number of people. I expected maybe fifty. Must be almost two hundred.

Mr. Krupowicz introduces me, says how proud he is, and all of Middletown should be, of a young man who has done such remarkable things. I'm embarrassed and proud that he says these things but can think of nothing to say. When he gives me an official plaque, leads the applause, I thank him and shake his hand and look at my mom grinning like crazy, applauding as much as anyone. And then the lights go down.

Click. The first slide. *Yaks on the way to Everest '96. Sherpas and dirt trail, deep blue sky, timeless.* I merely say, "This is how we travel to Base Camp. Two weeks at yak speed." And explain what yak speed is.

Click. Second slide. *A shot of Everest from a lower peak. Towering blacks, whites, and grays, and wispy snow plume.* "Taken from the trail to Base Camp." Something's happening inside my head. I can feel that my voice is flat, that I'm distracted somehow. I show more slides. The audience is still, mesmerized by the colors of the Nepali mountain scenes. But my tone sounds bored—just the opposite of what I feel. I want to tell them how alive I feel out there, how every day is such a new adventure, how wonderful it is to know that you can climb these huge mountains.

Click. Eighteenth slide. *Cho Oyu. Jabion and I, a day away from summit bid. White teeth sparkle from our dark faces. We lean together, ready for anything, full backpacks, ski poles, brilliant snow. A home of sorts.* "My friend Jabion and I at Camp Three on Cho Oyu." But there's so much more to say! Why can't I say it? Because if I try to, I might not be able to say anything. As I show these slides, I know more and more definitely that I'm not going to Everest in 1997. Been thinking about it for a couple of weeks, but now two things hit me at once. How much I love being there; how much I want to be with my father. And that's why I can't talk. Each slide is a sweet reminder, pulling me back to Nepal. Each slide is telling me: Enough; it's time to be a son now, not a climber.

Click. Slide 27. *An old Nepali woman sits in a doorway, prayer beads in hand, her face a swirl of wrinkles, her eyes full of mountains.* "A typical scene in a small Nepali village." To give up Everest will be very difficult in some ways. So many people know I plan to go, so many will think I'm quitting. I don't care what they think. Even my father wants me to go. That's always his way. Puts himself last. He'd help finance Everest '97. I told my mother we should spend any resources on getting Dad to Europe for experimental treatment, not on climbing. But they support any decision I make. They know this is my last chance for the record and all the potential sponsors for future climbs that go with it. "Just don't try to do Everest for anyone else," Dad says. "That can get you killed." So I'm not going. Couldn't be worrying about Dad and have the complete focus Everest demands at the same time. I have to call Henry tomorrow. I'll tell him no. I won't see any Nepali villages this year.

Click. Slide 37. *Ama Dablam. Night sky. A lacy white curtain of stars and meteors above the dark summit.* "My mother and I took night shots on Ama Dablam. And this is the result." Result? The stone-cold silence of utter darkness sprinkled with the phosphorescent glow of diamonds of light: that's Ama Dablam at night. Why can't I say that?

There's a certain sense of relief that I'm not going back. After I started climbing, I gradually began to narrow the focus of my life to Everest. It became, I must admit, all-consuming. Now, as I talk and show the slides, I can feel Everest's grip letting go, and so many things flood through my mind, parts of my life I've put aside. I can fish again. Not worry about calling sponsors. Even get a full night's sleep. I'll still work out with Paul Fletcher. Still run. And get back to being a teenager again.

The tunnel vision of focus has been good for me. It's taught me I can concentrate on one thing and make it happen. I talked to a sixth-grade class yesterday. The teacher asked me to give the kids one piece of advice. "Don't give up," I said. "Never give up. You want to do something and you think you can't? You can do it, if you put your mind to it. Stick with it." The teacher nodded; the kids didn't pay much attention. But that's what climbing gave me, the confidence to see something through.

Speaking of school, I don't know what to do. Too late now to start. Starting in January would give me some credits, but not nearly enough for me to go into my senior year in the fall. I know that after a while I'm going to feel very strange with neither climbing nor school as my focus.

Click. Slide 41. *Everest and Lhotse from Cho Oyu. Marbled peaks skirted with clouds, tranquil, inviting men to stand on the highest place on the planet. I will be there. Not now, but soon.* "You can see the South Col and the Hillary Step and the place where Camp Four would be." I can't say I will be there but not soon. I will just let it go.

I really want to talk about how the last three years have been like my pilgrimage to the mountains. I'd like to tell the audience that I looked up "religious pilgrimage" the other day and found out it involved separating yourself from your ordinary life, taking off on a journey full of hardship, and coming home, changed for life. I think my climbing fits that definition pretty well, especially the "changed for life" part. I'd like to be able to say all that and maybe someday I will, but right now I'll just show the sunset slides, ask if they have any questions, thank everyone for coming, go home, and tell my father that I'm not going to Everest, that I want to be here with him, that when I do go in '99, he'll be right here at home cheering me on. That much I do know.

DECEMBER 5, 1996

I'm standing outside the guidance office at Middletown High School, watching the rush of early-morning kids. It's a cold, gray day, and everyone who passes me looks as if he/she would rather be in a warm bed. Not me. It's great to be here. Wonderful. I see people I recognize. They wake up from their early-morning fog to wave, surprised but happy, it seems, to see me. I just met with my counselor and I asked if I could get back into school—now. She looked shocked at first, said she'd have to ask the principal, came back fifteen minutes later, smiling, and before I knew it, I had a schedule of classes. I had to take a lighter, less challenging course load than I would like; I had to promise to work on first-quarter material and catch up by the semester exams; I had to practically sign in blood that I'd be here for the rest of the school year. But I'm in. I'm a student again. Starting tomorrow! I can call my friend Mike, tell him I'll pick him up, and I'll go to school as if I never missed a beat.

More kids stream by on the way to first period. The girls I used to know in ninth and tenth grades look so much better now. I wonder why that is. I wonder, too, if I'll ever get the nerve to ask any of them out, like that small girl over near the main office who walks like a ballet dancer, or that one with the cute smile talking to a friend. And guys I hardly know come up to me, ask if I'm back in school. I say yes, and they seem glad that I am.

I made up my mind last night, got up early, and was here before seven, hoping to plead my case. I must admit, once I decided not to go to Everest, I felt like a high school dropout. I still worked out, helped out at home, and gave slide shows. But there was something missing. Kids my age belong in school—I belong in school—no doubt about it. I feel bad for all those people who have so little positive going on in their lives that all they can do is a negative: quit. It must be very lonely, and very hard to fill up your day, hard to feel as if you can do anything worthwhile. Kids my age need the direction that school can give us. A lot of it is boring, and some of it has no meaning at all, but at least it's a structure that you can learn in—if you want to.

Well, I sure want to learn. I want to take tough courses next year, graduate with my class, get my undergraduate degree, go on to medical school, and become an emergency-room doctor. And I will, too. Whatever discipline it takes, I know I can do it. Aconcagua taught me that. Ama Dablam taught me, and so did Everest and Cho Oyu. And Jabion, Al Burgess, and Henry Todd. Most of all, my father teaches me every day. Weird, isn't it? The guy who wanted only to stay home, to keep the home fires burning, is climbing the highest mountain, surviving the greatest storm, inside his own body. He's making it, too.

I know I'll climb more mountains, become involved in many other demanding physical activities, and I know I'll have to study hard for many years. But nothing can be any more challenging than the last three years. Those three years have made me ready for everything.

Right now I'm going to meet some of my teachers, get some books, and try to figure out how I can meet some of these girls. Cho Oyu and Everest were tough, but girls are going to be very difficult for a shy guy like me. Talk about a challenge!

EPILOGUE

On July 21, 1997, my dad died of complications from cancer. We had some great times together in his last months. He was in pain, but not bedridden; he even felt good enough to travel. So instead of keeping the home fires burning, Dad took our whole family, including Jabion, to Wyoming and then to Kentucky, where my dad grew up. He got to see his brothers for the first time in years and even visited some old high school buddies. He must have known something no one else knew, because when we came back home, it was only a matter of days before his last trip to the hospital.

I found that the best way for me to cope with my dad's death was to keep moving. Don't get me wrong: my life has a large hole in it. You can't lose your father, who happens to be your best friend, or your best friend, who happens to be your father, and live the same way you did before. But I'm not the sort of person who sits and broods or even discusses my feelings. I'd rather move. So I decided to take up scuba diving—something I'd never done with my dad, so

I knew I'd have no memories that could jump up and hit me all at once. I found that I love the quiet beauty underwater. I started working at a dive shop, trading hours for instruction and equipment, spending more and more time learning and diving.

At the dive shop I met Steve, a member of the elite Navy SEALs who had been a lead SEAL team climber in Peru. We decided to put together an Everest expedition. As the leader of this climb, I will be in charge of all logistics and preparation. After our climb we plan to explore the *Andrea Doria*, a cruise ship that sank 240 feet, off Cape Cod, and is now known as the "Everest" of deep-sea dives. Our trip will take us up Everest's 29,028 feet in May of 1999 and then down 240 feet to the *Andrea Doria* in late June or July.

Beyond next year's Everest-to-*Andrea Doria* trip, I plan to go to school and apply to either the Naval Academy or an ROTC program. After graduation I want to apply to the Naval Special Warfare Program. I also have an ongoing interest in medicine. I took another EMT course last fall and now have my certificate and want to take premed as an undergraduate. Medical school will be on the horizon after my Navy Special Warfare commitment.

The point is that I'm heading somewhere. Just as in mountain climbing, I'll put one foot in front of the other and keep going. Always climbing, training, exploring new ways to challenge myself.

I think my father would be proud.

CAST OF CHARACTERS

CHAPTER ONE

Geoff Tabin

Adventurer, author, doctor. Sparks Mark's interest in RI Rock Gym.

Frank Madeira

Symphony conductor, hiker. Introduces Mark to first hiking experience.

CHAPTER THREE

Al Burgess

Veteran leader of many Nepal treks and climbs. Mentor/leader of Nepal trek.

Eric and Hillary

Young couple from L.A., the other two members of trek group

Jabion, Lhakpa, Phurba, Pemba, Kami, Pasang

Sherpas

CHAPTER FOUR

Thor Keiser

Runs Condor Adventures. Accepts and encourages Mark to prepare for Everest through South American trips.

Aaron, Eleanor, Sterling   Fellow teenage participants in NOLS program

CHAPTER FIVE

Javier   Guide with Condor Adventures
"Butthead" (John)   Antagonistic member of Javier's small group
Inez   Cook
César   Local guide

CHAPTER SIX

Nel Poisson   Trainer who works Mark to new levels of fitness for Everest

CHAPTER SEVEN

Mr. Krupowicz   Assistant superintendent of Middletown Public Schools, instrumental in providing Mark with opportunities to pursue "alternative education"

ECUADOR TEAM

Gary   Gold dredger/California
Dean   Physicist/California
Tom   Doctor/Mississippi
Dave   Laser product engineer/Colorado
Louis   Lawyer/Connecticut
Greg   Fire jumper/Colorado
Javier   Leader
Luiz   Leader

Juan Carlos   Crazy driver

CHAPTER EIGHT

ACONCAGUA TEAM

Thor Keiser   Leader/Colorado
Javier
Pat Caffrey   Lumberjack/Montana
Tony Tonsing   Climber/Colorado

Carlo Rocca	Sixty-three-year-old survivor of triple-bypass surgery/California
Jim Wheeler	Neurologist/Colorado
George Fuller	Veteran climber/Colorado
Katarina Straskraba (Kat)	Skier, climber, Thor's girlfriend/Colorado
Kevin Burn	Doctor/Colorado

CHAPTERS NINE and TEN

EVEREST '95 TEAM

Thor Keiser*	Leader
Javier*	
Tony Tonsing*	
Jim Wheeler	Neurologist/Colorado
Kat	
Carlo Rocca	
Pat Caffrey	
Ray Dorr*	Veteran climber; set construction, Broadway shows/New York
Reinhardt Patscheider*	Experienced 8,000-meter climber; miraculously survived horrible fall on Annapurna/North Tirol
Greg Miller	Lawyer/California
Roger Gocking*	Veteran climber, college professor, long-distance runner, skier/Trinidad
Mike Roth*	Charter jet pilot/Colorado
Russell Brice*	Expedition leader, climber/New Zealand
John Tinker*	Climber/England
Motilal, Kashi ("Kami Kashi"), Pemba	Sherpas

CHAPTER ELEVEN

| Chris Fowler | ESPN sportscaster/New York |
| Drew Fowler | Chris's brother/New York |

*indicates previous experience on Everest

| Sean | Guide at Mount Rainier |
| Alison Hargreaves | First woman to summit Everest without oxygen. Died on K2. |

AMA DABLAM TEAM

Al Burgess	Leader/Utah
Travis Spitzer	Coleader/Colorado
Ace Kvale	Adventure photographer/Colorado
Anne Smith	Ace's girlfriend/Colorado
Allison Palmer	Physical therapist/England
Bob Mante	Engineer/Arizona
Phurba, Lhakpa	Sherpas

| Peter Habeler | Summited Everest without oxygen in 1978/England |

CHAPTER TWELVE

| Jeff Swimmer | TV producer filming Mark's Everest attempt/New York |

EVEREST '96 TEAM

Henry Todd*	Leader/Scotland
Jabion	
Ray Dorr*	
Brigeete Muir*	Climber/Belgium
Paul Deegan*	Outdoors instructor, Royal Air Force/England
Neil Laughton	Military/England
Graham Ratcliffe*	Auto mechanic/England
Thomas and Tina	Husband and wife/Sweden
Michael Jorgesen*	Military/Denmark

Göran Kropp	Solo climber/Sweden
Scott Fischer	Expedition leader of Mountain Madness/Washington
Anatoli Boukreev	Climber, guide with Mountain Madness/Russia and Kazakhstan

*indicates previous experience on Everest

CHAPTERS THIRTEEN and FOURTEEN

Rob Hall	Expedition leader of Adventure Consultants/New Zealand
Pete Athans	Veteran climber/Colorado
Neal Beidleman	Guide, aerospace engineer, ultramarathon runner/Colorado
David Breashears	Filmmaker, IMAX expedition leader/Massachusetts
Beck Weathers	Climber, doctor, severely injured survivor/Texas
Makalu Gau	Leader of Taiwanese expedition, survivor of storm/Taiwan
Yasuko Namba	Oldest woman to summit Everest/Japan
Andy Harris	Guide/New Zealand
Jabion, Pemba, Pasang, Ang Rita, Ang Tshering, Lhakpa, Kami	Sherpas

CHAPTER FIFTEEN

KILIMANJARO TEAM

Roger Gocking	Leader
Marion	Hiker, climber/Pittsburgh
Frank	Marion's husband/Pittsburgh
Phoebe	Marion's friend/Pittsburgh
Richard	Marion's thirteen-year-old son, whom Mark must "guide"/Pittsburgh
Fred	Philosophy student/Colorado
August	Local guide

CHAPTER SIXTEEN

CHO OYU TEAM

Henry Todd	Leader
Paul Fletcher	Mark's "Rambo" friend on first climb/Rhode Island
Larry	Lawyer/Chicago
Keith	Architect/Georgia
Chris	Keith's young wife/Georgia
Pavel	Polish engineer/South Africa

Ray Dorr
Anatoli Boukreev
Russell Brice
Jabion, Pemba,   Sherpas
Ang Tshering

Elizabeth Hawley   Unofficial media queen of all Everest
information/Kathmandu

GLOSSARY

BELAY—To secure a climber at one end of a rope to another climber at the opposite end of the rope. One climber remains stationary and feeds out the rope, stopping the feed with a mechanical brake if the other climber falls.

BETA—Rock-climbing term for essential information about moves on a particular climb

CARABINER—An oblong metal ring that is used to hold a freely running rope and also as a connector

CRAMPONS—Metal spikes worn on the bottom of mountaineering boots, usually having twelve points that dig into the ice for traction

CREVASSE—A crack or fissure in a glacier, which can be six inches or hundreds of feet deep and wide

DINNERPLATING—The shattering of hard and brittle ice that can occur when a climber strikes the mountain with an ice ax

DYNAMIC ROPE—A rope used by climbers that will stretch if a climber falls

HARNESS—A safety belt worn by a climber and attached to a rope to prevent falling

HYDRATION—Maintaining an adequate level of fluids in the body in order to avoid altitude sickness

ICE AX—A long bar with a spike at one end and a pick and hammer at the other; used in ice climbing and mountaineering for balance, anchoring, and self-arrest *(see below)*

ICE SCREW—A tubelike metal screw that is hammered, then screwed into the ice for protection. It has a metal hanger into which a carabiner is clipped. A rope is then clipped into the carabiner.

JUMAR—A mechanical hand-gripping device that is used to climb ropes more safely

PIANO MOVES—A hand-over-hand rock-climbing maneuver, which involves gradually replacing one hand with the other, one finger at a time, as a piano player would finger a scale on a keyboard

PITONS—Metal spikes or pegs that are hammered into rock to provide support and protection; most of the time they become permanent

PROTECTION—Safety equipment, such as ice screws, pitons, and snow stakes, that is attached to rock, snow, or ice in order to catch climbers if they fall

RE-RACK—The exchange of protection for climbers. (The second climber uses the leader's protection; when they meet, they exchange protection, and the leader then takes the second climber's protection to advance.)

SCREE—A slope of loose rock, sand, and dirt that is very difficult to climb because the surface crumbles with each step

SELF-ARREST—A technique that climbers use to stop from falling down a slope by digging an ice ax into the snow

SIRDAR—The "boss" Sherpa who works with the leader to organize the expedition. The sirdar determines all the activities of the Sherpas on his expedition team.

STATIC ROPE—A rope that is commonly used for jumaring and has no stretch

SWITCHBACK—A zigzag trail that cuts back and forth across a steep section. Although they add length, switchbacks make steep routes manageable.

TRAVERSING—Climbing across the face or slope of a mountain or rock, usually not gaining much altitude

UGLIES—Mark's nightly exercises of lying on his stomach and arching his back and lifting his legs. (He normally did 300 of these every night to strengthen his lower back.)

Mark Pfetzer holds several world records for high-altitude climbing, is a certified Emergency Medical Technician, and travels widely throughout the Northeast as a paid motivational speaker for audiences of all ages. He lives in Middletown, Rhode Island.

Jack Galvin is a freelance journalist who has written feature articles for many newspapers and magazines, including *Men's Fitness* and *Boston Magazine*. He lives in Providence, Rhode Island.